INSULT AND SOCIETY

INSULT
AND
SOCIETY

**Patterns of
Comparative Interaction**

Charles P. Flynn

National University Publications
KENNIKAT PRESS   //   1977
Port Washington, N. Y.   //   London

Manufactured in the United States of America

Published by
Kennikat Press Corp.
Port Washington, N. Y./London

Library of Congress Cataloging in Publication Data

Flynn, Charles P.
    Insult and society.

    (National university publications)
    Bibliography: p.
    Includes index.
    1. Invective. 2. Social interaction. I. Title
GT3070.F58   301.11   76-26973
ISBN 0-8046-9152-5

This book is dedicated to
Cornelia Toeppel Flynn and Anna Wentzel Wisott
Whose courage and faith have been an inspiration to me

CONTENTS

ACKNOWLEDGMENTS

Many people have helped both directly and indirectly in making this book possible. Foremost among the early influences upon my intellectual development were Herbert Blumer, Robert Blauner, and the late Ernest Becker, at the University of California in Berkeley; and Peter Berger, Harry Bredemeier, and Bernard Goldstein at Rutgers. I am very grateful to Goldstein for encouragement in the early stages of research for this book, particularly his suggestion for the use of the Human Relations Area Files as a source of data pertaining to insult behavior. Robert Atchley also provided substantial encouragement during the early stages of writing this book, and Wayne Fenner was extremely helpful in preparing the manuscript for publication. Thanks are also due to the staff of the Princeton University Library for allowing me full access to their collections of the Human Relations Area Files.

I would like to thank my wife, Betty, for helping in various ways, both in gathering material for the book and in providing a home atmosphere conducive to its completion.

INSULT AND SOCIETY

INTRODUCTION

An insult is an act, remark, or gesture which expresses a severely negative opinion of a person or group. But does its significance end with those who insult and are insulted?

Central to the sociological perspective is an assumption that behavior which appears to be limited to particular individuals or specific groups often has implications for the entire society in which it takes place. The microcosm of face-to-face interaction, including insult behavior, defines, supports, and maintains the macrocosm of the sociocultural order. And how an individual or group decides to respond to an insult may also help determine the transformation of a sociocultural system.

The purposes of this book are twofold: first, to study a wide variety of societies and cultures; second, to examine the connections between patterns of insult behavior and the sociocultural systems in which they take place. Societies often differ tremendously in what they consider an insult and in what their norms prescribe as proper responses to that insult. Studying such differences can often provide insights into the comparative characteristics of different types of sociocultural systems. We will examine insult patterns in three major kinds of sociocultural systems—tribal- village, caste-estate, and modern industrialized—to highlight some important differences in the patterns of insult behavior in these types of societies. Moreover, each chapter will deal with examples of insult behavior from each of these three major types of systems as they relate to a specific, central, social institution or social process. Thus, the book is intended not only to facilitate understanding of insult behavior, but also to afford a comparative study of sociocultural patterns and institutions from a new perspective and to examine and describe significant ways in which sociocultural systems which have been relatively neglected in previous social theory operate and maintain themselves.

Sources of Data

Since there have been few systematic studies of insult behavior, the data employed in this study come from a variety of sources. Most of the data were obtained from a thorough search of the Human Relations Area Files. All material directly or indirectly pertaining to insult behavior from different cultures was sorted into twenty-five categories, one of which was social stratification and insult. The available data thus obtained were analyzed according to the information they provided about the relations between the insult-related norms they described and the characteristics of the particular sociocultural systems involved. Since the Human Relations Area Files yielded data pertaining nearly exclusively to traditional cultures, and since there is a lack of systematic descriptive and analytical studies of insult behavior in modern cultures, it was necessary to rely upon a variety of sources to obtain material describing a variety of insult patterns in modern sociocultural systems. These non-systematic sources include: various historical, literary, and biographical accounts of incidents involving insult-related interaction; examples obtained from social scientific studies that do not focus upon the topic of insult; and personal accounts of insult-related encounters by informants, including minority group members.

Theoretical Perspectives

While the analyses of insult behavior in this book will draw upon a variety of theoretical perspectives, including behaviorism and structural functionalism, its primary theoretical orientations derive from two prominent schools of sociological thought and inquiry: symbolic interactionism and ethnomethodology.

Symbolic interaction regards human interaction as an ongoing creation of meaning by social actors, who, in the words of perhaps the foremost contemporary exponent of the approach, are not swept along as neutral and indifferent unit[s] by operation of a system. As organism[s] capable of self-interaction [social actors] forge their actions out of a process of definition involving choice, appraisal, and decision. Cultural norms, status positions, and role relationships are only frameworks inside of which that process of formative transaction goes on [Blumer, quoted by Buckley, 1967:21].

Most symbolic interactionist studies, however, have tended to place a strong emphasis on the social "microcosm," to the relative neglect of the sociocultural frameworks in which social interaction takes place. While Erving Goffman's analyses of norms of interaction have often focused upon the nature of the relationships between institutional settings (such as mental hospitals) and the manner and processes by which individuals present and maintain images of selfhood both to themselves and through interaction with others, his analyses have generally neglected to draw out the full extent of the ties between the "presentation of self" and the large-scale sociocultural frameworks in which the self is created and sustained in the process of face-to-face interaction. Thus, although this study is in the symbolic interactionist tradition, it is both more narrow and more encompassing than Goffman's studies: first, because it focuses on only one particular type of interactive behavior, and second, because it attempts to analyze how that behavior is related to a variety of large-scale sociocultural patterns, using a comparative approach which highlights the importance of cultural differentiation as well as the functional relationships between insult patterns and various kinds of sociocultural systems.

In addition to the symbolic interactionistic tradition, the present study is also related to the ethnomethodological approach, most strongly set forth and exemplified in the work of Harold Garfinkel. Garfinkel defines the purpose of ethnomethodology as uncovering the common sense perceptions of reality of people in everyday situations—what people in different cultures take for granted as "reality." These common understandings, according to Garfinkel, make social interaction, and, by extension, any sociocultural system, possible. Garfinkel is interested not only in people's actions, but in their knowledge of the world. A substantial part of this knowledge is what might be termed covert, as opposed to the overt, observable behavior of people engaged in social interaction. Thus, Garfinkel's quest is to understand "the ongoing accomplishments of organized artful practices of everyday life," the commonsensical, taken-for-granted, largely unspoken assumptions that underlie social behavior and that constitute the "knowledge" necessary for social interaction to take place [Garfinkel, 1967:11]. According to Cicourel, a major exponent of the ethnomethodological approach, its primary purpose is to understand the rules which govern social behavior by providing accounts of mundane activities [Cicourel, 1964:202]. The emphasis, however, is not upon the normative order itself, but rather upon actors' definitions of situations, "the prosaic details of everyday life upon which any . . . normative or moral structure logically depends" [McHugh, 1968:11]. It is the "informal," "unstated" understanding between people which provides the basis for the normative order, what McHugh refers to as the "bedrock" of the social order. Thus, the fundamental question of ethnomethodological research is "how does this abstraction (of shared understandings of the normative order) enter into the daily lives of individuals whose definitions are continually being made and remade?" [McHugh, 1968:12].

The covert nature of the rules that govern mundane activity renders them unobservable in a positivistic sense, largely because they are so much taken for granted by social actors that the rules are seldom if ever discussed in the normal course of social interaction. In order to uncover these covert, taken-for-granted, shared definitions of reality that underlie everyday behavior, Garfinkel and his fellow ethnomethodologists have engaged in research which deals primarily with the systematic breaking of established rules of conduct in mundane situations and the observation of people's reactions to such transgressions of normatively "proper" behavior. Perhaps the most noted example of such research involved Garfinkel's students, in conversation with others, breaking the taken-for-granted rules of proximity in social interaction by standing extremely close to them. In another research situation, students were asked to act like strangers in their own homes. In these, and in other research situations, Garfinkel and his associates observed that the unwitting subjects in the experiments reacted strongly against the transgression of taken-for-granted norms, as if they had been subjected to deliberate, direct insults. They expressed surprise, anger, and even hostility to the researchers. In many instances, the subjects' impressions that they had been insulted by the researchers were not dissipated even when the researchers explained the purpose of the experiment.

Our examination of insult behavior in this book is related in some respects to the ethnomethodological approach of Garfinkel and his associates. This book, then, will examine the nature of common, taken-for-granted assumptions concerning social reality shared by members of particular sociocultural systems, and show how insults in a wide variety of cultures consist largely of violations of these substantially unspoken but very significant norms. In many cultures, for example, adultery is a serious breach of the normative order and is thus considered a severe insult. In other cultures, immodesty of even a mild sort is severely insulting to anyone who happens to observe it, because of strong normative emphasis on the importance of modesty. A recurring purpose throughout this book is to show how insults—particular kinds of transgressions against the normative order of given cultures—contribute substantially to our understanding of the nature of taken-for-granted assumptions and of the conceptions of the social realities of various cultures. This purpose is essentially similar to the primary scientific goals of ethnomethodology stated by Garfinkel and others. The main distinction is in the means by which such understandings are obtained: in the present work, through analyses of ethnographic and related materials; in ethnomethodological studies, through the type of research studies described above, which often use insult as a means of uncovering underlying assumptions.

Despite its ties with the recently developed "traditions" of symbolic interactionism and ethnomethodology in sociological analysis, the analyses of insult behavior in this book are aimed at making more explicit the ties between social interaction involving insult, and the sociocultural frameworks in which such interaction takes place. Let us draw out, in the form of a model, the links between self, social-interactional settings, and sociocultural milieu that form the basis of the model of insult behavior in this book.

The individual social actor engages in continual self-response as he internalizes the anticipated reactions of others toward himself. In countless lectures, Herbert Blumer has described the socialized individual's continual process of self-interaction: "The self is an object unto itself; the human individual is uniquely capable of self-interaction."

In human social interaction, the individual is continually obtaining response from others and providing various kinds of response to those with whom he interacts. In the model to be used here, the ongoing process of interaction between two or more individuals takes place on two levels: the overt and the covert. Overt interaction refers to the manifest contents of verbal communication between interactants. In a simple example, one individual proposes an idea, and the other, approving of it, states, "Say, that's a great idea! I'm sure that'll work out fine." Or, alternatively, the listener might disapprove of the idea and offer negative overt response: "Well, I don't know. I don't think that would be much of an improvement." In either case, the response is clearly positive or negative, and is expressed openly. Most interaction, however, involves a more subtle giving and receiving of response, in which the actors for various reasons do not openly express their attitudes. Covert interaction thus involves the various kinds of subtle, unspoken, but very real types of response and counter-response which are continually going on under the surface, so to speak, of the manifest, or overt interaction. Covert interaction thus refers to two kinds of interaction: that which is subtly communicated through general demeanor, gesture, tone of voice, and so on; and the continual evaluative dialogue which takes place within the minds of the individual actors, where they not only make indications to themselves about the other person or persons but continually attempt to ascertain what the other is thinking about them.

The significance of covert interaction is that it is primarily on the covert level that the true meanings of the interaction are created. These meanings may or may not be mutually conveyed to one another by the interactants. For example, a man and woman may be conversing, and the man may find the woman sexually attractive, or vice versa. Under some circumstances, it would be normatively "proper" for the man to make some indication of his feelings. He might do so overtly: if she says, "That music is very beautiful," he may use this as an opening and reply in a certain manner, "You're very beautiful, too." This makes overt the previously covert interaction that had been taking place all along, hopefully leading toward positive response from the girl, who may either accept or reject the implied overture. In this typified instance, as in most instances of interaction, the desire of the interactants is that mutual, reciprocal positive response will take place. In the example of the dating couple, if they are attracted to one another they will respond to one another with mutual positive response. At the same time, of course, the response of the girl might be negative: she may covertly reject the amorous advances, or may overtly offer strong negative response, e.g., "You disgust me." The latter, a strong instance of negative response, is always possible in any instance of interaction. It is an example of insult.

One of the most important characteristics of insult is not only that it is a type of interaction, but that it is never dependent wholly upon the manifest overt content of a communication. Put in symbolic-interactionist terms, insult is created through a particular, mutual definition of a remark or other communication. Thus, the definition of an act or remark as insulting is always dependent upon the shared sets of cultural meanings of the interactants, what ethnomethodologists term "shared conceptions of social reality." These meanings may be conveyed, once again, either overtly or covertly. The central importance of the covert level of analysis in interaction involving insult is that it is often the unstated gesture or tone of voice, rather than the overt, manifest content of a statement or act, which determines an insult. Thus, by relying on the cultural meanings transmitted by tone of voice, covert insults may be given by members of one culture to those of another culture that does not share these meanings:

[Among the Yoruba] the use of the proper form of address is not in itself sufficient to show respect for a person of superior status; the tone of the speaker's voice is equally important. The Yoruba delight in insulting Europeans without fear of reprisal by employing a complimentary form of address spoken in a tone which shows disrespect and contempt, but which the Europeans fail to recognize as insolence [Bascom, 1942: 45-46].

This example of the importance of the covert level of analysis is also exemplary of the relationship between insult and socioeconomic status, a topic with which we will deal fully later on. But in a more general sense, it also shows the close connection between insult behavior and the socio-cultural system, the macrocosm, in which the behavior takes place. First, as both symbolic interactionists and ethnomethodologists correctly observe, an insult is the product and the creation of actors. But these actors must also, as Blumer recognizes, rely upon a framework of cultural meanings from which the meaning of their interaction derives. Moreover, the macrocosm (or system, if you will) interposes itself in any interaction involving insult by: (1) in many cases helping to determine the motivations underlying the individual insult (e.g., in the Yorubas' evident desire to "undercut" the superior-inferior status relation between themselves and the Europeans); (2) providing a repertoire of cultural meanings, both overt and covert, so that a situation, act, or remark might be defined as insulting; and (3) by setting forth both expectations and limitations pertaining to the permissible kinds of response to insult for which the object of an insult will obtain positive response.

Factors Related to Patterns of Response to Insults

One of the important aspects of insult behavior involves patterns of response to insult. Assuming that an insult is communicated to its object, the recipient is always motivated to respond in some manner, even though the response may be internal and hence not apparent to others. The motivation to respond to insult lies in the fact that insult is a particular, and serious, type of negative response. Since the individual seeks to maintain positive response both from others and from himself (reflexive response that internally anticipates positive response from others), the occurrence of an insult constitutes a break in the ongoing flow of positive response. Put differently and in more conventional terms, the individual strives to maintain a sense of self-regard and self-esteem. Insult is a direct negation of this that abruptly cuts off and reverses the flow of positive response, both external and reflexive. Hence, insult almost always causes a subjective reaction: anger, hurt feelings, and the like, which are nothing more than the subjective component of the interruption and negation of the flow of positive response. In effect, the basis of the individual's positive response has been thrown off balance and if he is to regain that flow he must respond to the insult in some manner. How he responds is in some measure dependent upon his temperamental inclinations. But even more significant are the expectations and prescriptions of the socio-cultural system of which he is part. In some cultures, response to insult is a major way in which the salient cultural values as well as individual and family honor are defined and maintained. In Parsonian terms, response to insult is a central mechanism of pattern maintenance, as well as the maintenance of individual reputation and self-regard. The way in which response to insult may serve as a dominant means of sustaining the kinds of character traits necessary for group survival, as well as sustaining the values related to these traits, is well illustrated by the Zagori, a mountain people of Greece.

The community will gradually form an opinion of [a young man's] prowess as a shepherd, his fearlessness on the high ridges, his devotion to a sick or injured sheep, and his skill in grazing. But the critical moment in the development of a young shepherd's reputation is his first quarrel. Quarrels are necessarily public. They may occur in the coffee-shop, the village square, or most frequently on a grazing boundary where a curse or stone aimed at one of his straying sheep by another shepherd is an insult which inevitably requires a violent response. In any case some account of the event becomes public property. . . . It is the critical nature of these first important tests of his manliness that makes the self-regard of the young shepherd so extremely sensitive. It is not only the reality of an obvious insult which provokes him to action, but even the finest allusions on which it is possible to place some unflattering construction. It may be possible to recover from an early failure of nerve and conduct, but a series of failures is fatal to a man's reputation [Campbell, 1964:280-81].

In this example all three levels of analysis that we have discussed previously are apparent: the self (microcosm) seeking to maintain positive response both from the community (reputation) and internally (self-regard); the interactional setting in which acts and remarks are defined as insulting and in which the actors create the meanings of their actions; and the socio-cultural system, which prescribes strong response to insult in order to maintain the behavioral patterns and character traits necessary for the survival of the Zagori. No one theoretical perspective alone is sufficient to fully account for and illuminate the nature of insult and response among the Zagori. When the behaviorist, symbolic-interactionist, and structural-functionalist approaches are employed in combination, it is possible to obtain a fuller understanding of a given social phenomenon.

To this point the theoretical exposition has been relatively unsystematic; hence the remaining portion of this section will be devoted to setting forth in detail the specific theoretical model which will be used in the analysis of insult behavior. As indicated previously, the model posits three primary levels of analysis: self, interactional context, and social system. Insult and response behavior takes place on each level in the following ideal-typical manner:

The self, during the course of socialization, internalizes the values, norms, and role expectations of the sociocultural system. The self seeks to maximize positive and minimize negative response. Through the internalization process and through the reactions of significant others toward it within the interactional context, the self becomes a social object unto itself. In this way, the individual becomes capable of reflexive response— he is able to reward and punish himself for his own and anticipated behavior. As an extreme instance of negative response, insults directed at the self require response in order to maintain ongoing positive response from others (honor, reputation) and from self (self-esteem, self-respect).

On the interactional level, acts and remarks are situationally defined as insults through culturally shared meanings communicated either overtly (in the manifest, abusive content of acts or remarks) or covertly (through subtle gestures, tone of voice, and so on).

The sociocultural system provides the framework within which actors create and define acts and remarks as insults, on the basis of shared cultural meanings. Moreover, norms of the definition of and response to insults are functionally related to the maintenance of the system.

1

CULTURAL DIFFERENCES IN INSULT BEHAVIOR

Culture has been described as the total way of life of a group—its total design for living. A significant part of this total design consists of a set of shared meanings upon which the members of a social system can relate both to the physical reality around them, and to one another. Language is the most pervasive mechanism by which cultural meanings are transmitted; it provides a basic medium for individuals to coordinate their actions. In every culture, however, there are many nonsymbolic media such as acts, gestures, tones of voice, and facial expressions that convey varied meanings which vary considerably from culture to culture. Here we are interested specifically in the expression of insult.

Central to the sociological perspective is the idea that what is right or proper in one culture may be wrong or improper in another. This differentiation of values and normative patterns is clearly manifest in the wide discrepancies between cultures, both in the kinds of acts and remarks that are considered insulting, and in the types of responses prescribed by the normative order for an offended person to deal with an insult directed against him.

Varieties of Insults

Acts, expressions, gestures, and remarks that are totally innocuous, even friendly, in one culture may constitute grave insults in another. For example, in certain tribal cultures in Nigeria, to raise one's hand toward another, much as Americans would wave "Hi!" in greeting, is considered a very serious insult. In the Nigerian culture, such a gesture suggests that the sexual organs of the parents of the person to whom the gesture is directed are diseased. This is a very striking example of the manner in which virtually identical gestures can have totally opposite meanings in different cultures [Emmanuel Shittu, personal communication].

Among the Ashanti, an African tribe, it is particularly insulting to put out the left hand to take anything from another. It is also insulting to point out a thing with the left hand. The reason for this lies in the fact that the left hand, never the right, is used to hold the stick with which the Ashanti generally wipe the anus. In the Ashanti culture, then, the use of the left hand has a particular cultural meaning not found in most other cultures [Rattray, 1916:175].

Another African tribe, the Fang, regard any question concerning their full names (i.e., their surnames) as insulting. Even worse to the Fang is any mention, by an outsider, of his ancestors. The extreme sensitivity of the Fang in this regard can be explained by the fact that their families, including their ancestors, are the basic source of their individual pride and collective self-esteem. Accordingly, even the mention of a surname or ancestor is, to the Fang, an implicit threat to his family, since it involves the possibility of criticism [Tessman, 1913:155]. Similar sensitivity to the mentioning of surnames and ancestors is found in other societies in which the extended family is the central social institution, such as in traditional China.

It is an insult to ask a Yoruba tribesman "Why are you cooking?" if he happens to be cooking his own food. The Yoruba sensitivity in this regard is related to the normative patterns of the Yoruba culture: for fear of gossip and ridicule, Yoruba men do not cook for themselves. It would be assumed that they were either so bad that their wives and their close female relatives refused to cook for them, or that they were so miserly that they were trying to save a little that their wives were trying to waste [Bascom, 1951:50].

Until relatively recent times, cannibalism was part of Samoan tribal society. One implication of the existence of cannibalism was that certain acts, remarks, or gestures were very offensive because they carried cultural meanings different from those found in cultures that do not condone cannibalism. For example, if a person seated in a house called for some food to eat as he saw another person approaching, the second person was immediately offended because it was considered to be equivalent to asking for vegetables to eat with the body of the approaching person. Or, if an individual seated in a house wanted a knife, and asked for one to be brought to him without first offering an apology to any person who might be seated near him, a grievous insult was offered, since it was assumed that the offending person had called for a knife or hatchet with which to cut up the body of the person sitting near him. Or if a coconut were broken in a house by a person at the time that another was approaching, the act was considered an insult because it implied that the offender was expressing a desire to break the approaching person's head. A similar cultural meaning was attached to chopping wood or any similar kind of work involving beating: Samoans who wished to avoid giving offense were obliged to cease such work every time a person passed, since to continue would be regarded as equivalent to beating or wishing to mutilate the person passing [Stair, 1897:125].

Although all the preceding examples of cultural differentiation refer to so-called primitive societies, such variations in what is considered insulting are very apparent in other kinds of sociocultural contexts. In many parts of contemporary Latin America, for example, it is considered very insulting for a person, if asked for a match, to give a lighted cigarette or cigar butt to the other and then leave him with the butt. In North America such a gesture would at most be considered mildly tactless, if indeed it had any negative connotations at all. In modern Iran, if a person has been offered some beverage in a cup or glass, the rudest insult which he can make is to return the receptacle after he has drunk. In America, not to return the glass would most probably be considered bad manners [Masse, 1938:271].

One can readily see that lack of knowledge of the cultural meanings of other cultures could very easily lead to trouble for an outsider who might inadvertently proffer insults. Such problems were encountered by Americans who occupied the Truk Islands of the South Seas during and for a few years after the Second World War. Among the Trukese, it is a grave insult to wake a person violently; the proper technique is to repeat softly over and over again the sleeper's name [Gladwin and Sarason, 1953:59]. Obviously, the Americans' use of army bugles to awaken their Trukese helpers insulted and alienated them.

Contrasting patterns of what is considered insulting may often be explained by related contrasts not only in cultural meanings, but also in basically opposite value and normative standards. Again, this is apparent in differing patterns of insult content among not only primitive peoples, but also in modern societies. In parts of Greece, for example, to accuse someone of being a liar is not the gross insult it is in the United States. The reason for this difference lies in the Greek attitude toward truth and falsehood, which is quite different from that of the American culture. In Greek village culture, some form of deception as a means of achieving a particular good is acceptable as a technique for conducting one's affairs in the village or with outsiders. Each man and woman expects to develop skills both in the art of guilefulness and in the art of detecting guilefulness in others. Thus, in contrast to middle-class American standards, mendacity is valued in Greek culture [Friedl, 1963:80].

Another example of how contrasting cultural standards are directly related to contradictory definitions of what is insulting can be seen in the fact that it is as seriously offensive for a Yuma Indian girl to be called "skinny" as it is for a woman of the dominant American culture to be described as "fat." The discrepancy, of course, is in differing values; for the Yuma, "the fatter the better," while for the American white woman, obesity is culturally defined anathema [Smithson, 1959:72].

Are There Culturally Universal Insults?

Despite the many differences that exist between cultures as to what is considered insulting, there are certain kinds of remarks and acts which are offensive in so wide a range of cultures that they might be regarded as universal insults. Since the examples thus far have been selected to highlight cultural differentiation, here we must counterbalance the preceding emphasis to make the point that there are similarities as well as differences in acts and remarks which otherwise widely disparate cultures define as insulting. The words *dog* and *pig*, for example, are very common terms of abuse in most societies, from the most primitive tribal village culture to the most modern industrialized context. In the primitive society of the African Bambara tribe, for example, to call a man a son of a dog is enough to throw him into a fit of extreme anger and desire for revenge [Henry, 1910:7]. In traditional Malaysian society, a Malay is always careful not to use the terms *dog* or *pig* in scolding or rebuking a wrongdoer unless he is very angry and ready for a fight. If, on the other hand, he himself is called a dog or pig he will, like the Bambara, "see red" at once and will, if he can, commit violence on his reviler to show that he is not such an animal [Ahmad, 1950:69]. In America, "son of a bitch" is still considered a very serious insult if uttered in a serious manner; and to call someone a pig is a common American abuse, most recently used to insult police officers.

Spitting is another common, virtually universal insult. In many societies, including our own, spitting at or in the direction of someone constitutes a grave affront. In Malaysia, as in America and many other cultures, spitting, if done deliberately with a certain amount of force and impatience and accompanied by an angry irritated look, is an emphatic expression of hatred and contempt for a person, even if nothing is said or spoken to that effect. The act of spitting in this manner has virtually identical meaning in many other cultures that are widely divergent in other respects. In Malaysian society as well as in many other contexts, spitting at a person or in his face is one of the very worst insults. Thus, in many if not most societies, one must be careful not to do any spitting that could be interpreted as slights or intentional show of disrespect to the people near him [Ahmad, 1950:65].

Sex and Obscenity—Social Universals

Perhaps no type of insult is so widespread and occurs in as wide a variety of cultures as the use of obscenity. From the most primitive tribal culture to the most complex industrialized society, obscene gestures and remarks, together with allegations and insinuations of sexually nonconforming behavior, are a very common vehicle for the expression of insult. Moreover, the content of sex-related insults in different cultures is clearly related to the sexual mores of the society. Thus, the severity of an obscene insult in any given culture is dependent on the degree of salience of the norm which the insulted person is accused of transgressing. In cultures, for example, where the incest taboo is the most salient element of its normative code, any insinuation that someone has been or is engaging in incestuous behavior will constitute a most severe insult. Since the incest taboo is a central component of the sexual mores of both primitive and modern societies, incest-related insult is found in a wide variety of cultures, if not universally. A good example of the relation between insult and the sexual code of a primitive culture is afforded by Powdermaker's study of the Lesu tribe of New Ireland. Among the Lesu, insulting terms and obscene phrases used in quarrels are frequently concerned with forbidden incestuous relationships. "You copulate with your sister" is the very worst insult that one Lesu can fling at another [Powdermaker, 1933:270]. A similar pattern is found among both the Nkundu and the Hottentots. To the Nkundu, crude language is especially reprehensible and wounding if it contains allusions to incest [Hulstaert, 1928:49-51]. The worst Hottentot insults are those which not only offend one's modesty but also one's sense of piety, since they are aimed not only at the insulted person but also his mother or his sister. "Go sleep with your sister" is an insult which will make even the most passive Hottentot furious [Schultze, 1907:119].

In modern industrialized societies, accusations of incest are also a common form of abuse. The term *motherfucker* is prevalent among ghetto youth, particularly as a means of abuse against unpopular figures, including whites and police. In modern American culture, insults involving incest are likely to be taken as seriously as in many primitive societies.

Another very common type of sex-related insult found in wide varieties of cultural contexts is the abusive reference to sexual organs and sexual functions. The use of genital references as insults are common in primitive and modern industrialized societies. Among the Lesu, for example, obscene expressions used in quarrels refer directly to the sexual organs: such expressions as "red vagina," "black vagina," "you big penis," and so on, are common insults [Powdermaker, 1933:271]. Again, the degree of severity of genital-related insults is a direct function of the degree to which abusive genital references offend and transgress a given culture's norms of modesty. Among the Hottentots, insults which offend the value of modesty, such as the common "you with the big penis," are considered fighting words even by the least prudish person [Schultze, 1907:121]. Among the Marquesans of the Pacific, there is an extreme normative emphasis on genital cleanliness. Accordingly, the most severe insults are those which insinuate that the offended person has unclean genitals. An expression of this relationship between cultural emphasis and insult-content is found in the fact that the insult "your stinking foreskin filth" is an extremely serious affront when uttered in anger [Suggs, 1971:172].

In some cultures, sexual modesty is such an important value that even the least lapse of modesty in the presence of another constitutes a gross insult. Winstedt has observed that in Malayan society, a person's willful exposure to another in an indecent manner is the most severe affront with which one Malay can insult another [Winstedt, 1925:6]. In Malaya, the exceptionally strong cultural emphasis on modesty has at times led to extreme consequences for those who transgress the norms of modesty even slightly. A Malayan chief, for example, fined a man $100 for lifting the ends of his trousers clear of the mud as he passed in front of the chief's house. The norms governing sexual modesty are also strong in many other primitive societies, such as the Guajiro Indian culture. The Guajiro woman, even if she is a prostitute, never acts immodestly, since there is no greater insult than that a man should accuse her of showing herself naked [Pineda Giraldo, 1950:124].

The Functions of Modesty—Women's Power

Contrasted with most modern societies, the extreme emphasis placed upon sexual modesty in many primitive and traditional cultures is an important distinction. In present-day American culture, insults with a reference to the genitalia are common, but for the most part are not defined as serious affronts. The common gesture of raising the middle finger to symbolize an erect penis, with the meaning of "fuck you," is occasionally defined as a serious insult, but for the most part amounts to nothing more than the bantering of adolescent boys. Perhaps a more significant contrast between modern American and some primitive and traditional societies is in the relative seriousness of insults that accuse the offended person of immodesty. As we have seen, such affronts are very serious indeed in many primitive and traditional contexts. But in modern America and Western Europe, revealing clothing styles and even occasional collegiate "streaking"—exposure which would be considered shameful and insulting in many other societies—are condoned and perhaps even encouraged. Why this discrepancy between modern American and many other cultures in their valuation of modesty? And why is immodesty considered extremely insulting in many societies but not in our own?

One explanation, at least for norms of modesty governing women, is that in many primitive and traditional societies, women's genitals are a basic source of their power. Strong prohibitions against immodest behavior arise as a necessary means of protection of women's physical basis of power. More specifically, women in many primitive and traditional societies adhere to extreme norms of modesty so as not to expose their assets to their competitors. From the point of view of modern American culture, this use of genitals is difficult to understand—perhaps because our cultural disposition is to view sexual modesty as having a religious value rather than a functional basis relating to social power. In direct contrast to the use of modesty to protect their source of power, many modern American women are willing to forego modesty in order to gain power and prestige (e.g., movie starlets, *Playboy* playmates, and so on). But regardless of how odd such uses of modesty may seem from our own cultural perspective, there are still many primitive and traditional societies in which women's modesty, rather than immodesty, is directly and functionally related to the manner in which they establish and maintain social power. Among the Yap Islanders of the South Seas, for example, a woman's genitals have the same connotations as a man's land; they are her "real" assets with which she maintains her position in the Yap hierarchy of rank and prestige. A Yap woman relies on her genitals to get what she wants: lovers, attention, and power over men, all of which mitigate her subservient position [Muller, 1917:332].

The cultural definition of genitals as a basis of women's social power is clearly evident in the society of the Trukese, where the greater modesty of women as compared to men is directly related to the genital competition in which women often engage as a way of attempting to humiliate and insult one another. If two Truk women get into a bitter argument, their final insult is to accuse one another of having vaginas with nothing in them. Both women would then strip off their skirts and the onlookers would pass judgment on the relative merits of the competitors' genitals. The woman who proved inferior was deeply humiliated, for she was defined as inferior not only in a physical sense but in terms of social prestige and power. Thus, the Truk norms of modesty protect the Truk woman's basis of social power by not exposing her to invidious comparison, and hence saving her from possible insult and humiliation [Gladwin and Sarason, 1953:288].

In some cultures, women deliberately break the norms of modesty in order to insult someone and to exercise social power. In such instances, women who wish to show their vehement rejection of some individual or group deliberately exhibit their genitals by removing their undergarments, standing in line with their backs to the offender, bending forward, and lifting their skirts in unison. This use of the genitals as a vehicle of insult is found among the Kikuyu tribe of East Africa. With this gesture, which is usually directed against a man or against another group of women, Kikuyu women indicate either that they will have no further social dealings with the people they have insulted, or that they do not recognize the authority of the man who has been the object of their affront. At times, the skirt-raising gesture has been employed in a most solemn manner by all the women of a Kikuyu tribal subgroup to indicate their hostility toward another subgroup [Lambert, 1956:99].

2

CULTURAL VARIATIONS
IN RESPONSE TO INSULT

Norms governing socially proper response to insult also vary significantly from one culture to another. At this point, let us examine some of the often striking contrasts between cultures in their normative prescriptions for responding to insults.

In general, societies that prescribe violent retaliations for an affront from their individual members exhibit a value system which places a strong emphasis both on individual and group honor. As shall be discussed more fully in a later chapter, European feudal aristocracies such as the Prussian Junkers develop in their young men a strong sense of class-related honor; in such societies any affront must be violently avenged. On the individual level, this cultural pattern means that the Prussian Junker is extremely "touchy" and is likely to perceive an insult when one is not necessarily intended. Such touchiness is by no means confined to European upper classes, but can be found in many primitive and traditional cultures. Among the Tlingit, for example, violent revenge is the normal response to any insult; an affront is never forgotten or forgiven until in some way it has been avenged [Jones, 1914:96]. Similarly, the Yapese are said to have a "good memory" for slights they have suffered. The Yap is resentful of an insult for years afterward, watching for an opportunity to obtain satisfaction [Salesius, 1907:60].

In Greek peasant culture, the individual, from his earliest years, is imbued with the concept of *philotimo*, or individual honor. The essence of philotimo is inviolability. This means that the Greek villager is typically very touchy. Moreover, any insult or affront constitutes an attack upon a person's philotimo, and calls for immediate, violent retaliation. Such violence is usually of an informal character; that is, it does not conform to any ritualized pattern but consists, rather, of a spontaneous physical attack upon an offender [Lee, 1953:5]. In other traditional societies, such as the American South of the nineteenth century, the violent response was highly formalized in the institution of duelling, which will concern us in a later chapter.

Nonviolent and Passive Response to Insult

Whereas some cultures socialize their members to welcome insults so as to provide them with a test of strength and defense of honor, other societies strive to inhibit intragroup aggression of all kinds, and likewise prescribe nonviolent or passive modes of response in the event of an insult. Interestingly enough, the tendency of some societies to de-emphasize aggression and active response to insults is directly related to certain conditions of an objective nature which would make it virtually impossible for the society to survive if violent response to insult were to occur frequently between significant numbers of individuals. African Bushmen, for example, cannot afford to fight with each other and almost never do because their only real weapon is the poison arrow, for which there is no antidote. Thus, a Bushman will go to great lengths to avoid insulting other Bushmen [Marshall, 1961:231-32].

In other cultures, minimization of response is not necessarily linked to any particular circumstances but is simply a part of a general value emphasis upon nonviolence and lack of sensitivity to insult. Among the Tewa Indians of South America, for example, overt acts of hostility are suppressed to such an extent that the average individual will go out of his way to avoid an open quarrel. It is not considered a disgrace to walk away from a quarrel, nor is it an insult to call another man a coward. In fact, the feeling against quarreling is so strong that it takes a physical act of hostility to insult a man, such as striking or pushing him. As an old Tewa said: "If an old man insults you with words, he may be joking." The desire of the Tewa to avoid hostility extends even to legal matters. In one instance, one Tewa built a house on land owned by another, but the latter was unwilling to take legal action or to respond in any way because "it might cause a fight" [Whitman, 1947:54].

The norms of some other societies do not inhibit insults, but do prescribe withdrawal rather than violent retaliation as the proper mode of response. In an early account of the natives of the Aleutian Islands, a Russian ethnographer states that the Aleuts will never seek satisfaction for any injury done to them. When offended or irritated, they would fall silent and withdraw from the offender [Veniaminov, 1840:55]. Similarly, in the traditional society of Thailand, private disputes and insults are typically passed off without violence. In the midst of an altercation, one party will suddenly turn his back on the whole thing. As one Thai stated, "The best way to show your opponent up is to give in to him. Anger is the least advantageous method of meeting a difficult situation" [Benedict, 1952:57].

The Aleuts and the Thai are thus able to "shrug off" insults so that a chain of revenge and counterrevenge is avoided. There are certain other cultures with nonviolent norms, however, in which mere withdrawal is not sufficient to end the matter. In these cultures, violent response against an offender is not acceptable, but suicide is.

Suicide as a Response to Insult

In societies where suicide is a proper, even expected, mode of response to insult, the act has a different cultural meaning than that with which Euro-Americans are familiar. Suicide as a form of response to insult typically serves to punish an offender indirectly by causing him to be ostracized by his neighbors. In traditional China of the prerevolutionary era, for example, suicide was not only the sole acceptable means of response to insult, but also the mode of retaliation most likely to cause the offender to suffer. While the traditional Chinese regarded the use of physical violence as a breach of good breeding, they considered suicide an honorable means of protest. By committing suicide, the aggrieved party brought social disapproval upon the one who had insulted him, and caused the offender embarrassment with officials and neighbors [LaTourette, 1934:212].

A similar use of suicide is apparent in the insult-response norms of the Matako, a South American Indian culture. Among the Matako, suicide is the sole acceptable means of retaliating against an offender. The Matako culture attaches a decidedly aggressive meaning to the act of suicide; by killing themselves, they punish the person who has offended them. Moreover, Matako culture strongly inhibits direct aggression against others. Ethnographers have traced this cultural tendency to the influence of missionaries, who were successful in suppressing all direct outlets for aggression, such as sports, drinking, warfare, and the like. As a result of having become successfully socialized to the nonaggressive values and norms of the missionaries, modern Matako society has no institutionalized mechanism for a person to give direct vent to his feelings of anger and aggression. Ironically, suicide is the only way to punish an offender [Metraux, 1943:209].

In addition to missionary-bred values which cause some societies to prescribe suicide as a proper mode of response to insult, a more typical reason for suicide as a response to insult is evident in many cultures' strong taboos against intrafamilial aggression. Among the Paiute Indians of North America, for example, direct aggressive response against a member of one's family is simply unthinkable. Accordingly, Paiute wives typically commit suicide when their husbands have abused and insulted them. The Paiute pattern of inhibition of direct aggression also extends outside the family and is inculcated from early childhood. The child is instructed not to be aggressive toward his family or other people, to love his parents, and to be pleasant to outsiders. He observes that his parents are afraid to express aggression and that they show guilt about having mean thoughts. All of this serves to internalize in the child a very strong disinclination to respond violently against an insulter and a corresponding acceptance of suicide as the only possible mode of response. Needless to say, such a culturally induced response predisposition is completely contradictory to the values and norms of many other cultures [Whiting, 1950:70-72].

The type of response considered appropriate for various kinds of insults is as culturally differentiated as the kinds of acts and remarks that are regarded as insulting. Moreover, the severity of the insult, together with the vehemence of the response it elicits, is directly related to the degree to which the insult involves accusations that the offended party has transgressed serious cultural mores. In most cases the more serious the norm that the insulted person is accused of violating, the more serious the insult and the more vigorous the prescribed mode of response. Adultery, for example, is in most societies considered both a serious offense against moral standards and an insult against an offended spouse.

Insult and Adultery

The degree to which adultery is considered insulting is related to the degree of permissiveness of the cultural norms governing extramarital relationships. Among very conservative peoples, such as the Guajiro Indians of South America, not only adultery but also the discovery by a husband that his wife was not a virgin at marriage constitutes a grave insult. Because of the strong valuation placed upon virginity at marriage, a Guajiro bride will often resort to deception so that her husband, on their wedding night, will believe that she is a virgin. When the husband, through friends' gossip and other means, discovers later that he has been deceived, he reacts with anger against the severe insult, often insulting his wife in public and even violently attacking her. For example, in drunken bouts with his friends, the disillusioned Guajiro husband will often insult and degrade his wife, using grossly insulting vulgarities in order to express the depth of his feelings of anger and resentment. He may even go so far as to make up obscene songs containing references to his wife's premarital escapades and will sing them to his wife in front of his friends in order to humiliate her. The wife, realizing her socially disadvantageous situation, seldom protests [Pineda Giraldo, 1950:50] .

In more permissive societies, a completely opposite attitude toward adultery is sometimes apparent. Ruesch relates how an Eskimo husband can be highly insulted and respond in a lethally violent manner when a guest refuses to accept the Eskimo husband's offer to spend a night with the host's wife. As the Eskimo Ernenek explains in Ruesch's fictionalized account based on ethnographic research,

"I was right in killing him. He insulted my wife abominably. . . . She had purposely groomed herself! And what did the white man do? He turned his back to her! That was too much! Should a man let his wife be ·so insulted?"
"Refusing isn't fitting for a man!" Ernenek said indignantly. "Anybody would rather lend out his wife than something else. Lend out your sled and you'll get it back cracked, lend out your saw and some teeth will be missing, lend out your dogs and they'll come home crawling, tired— but no matter how often you lend out your wife she'll always stay like new" [Ruesch, 1950:79; 104–5] .

In a classic article on the nature of jealousy, Kingsley Davis offers some insights into how and why such opposing orientations toward adultery can lead to similar reactions from husbands who regard themselves as having been offended, albeit for opposite reasons. According to Davis, a love object, such as a wife or lover, can be considered a type of noneconomic property. As such, its possessor is subject to the "dangers that beset any person with regard to property," specifically, "that somebody will illegitimately take from him property already acquired. This is the danger of trespass" [Davis, 1936:396]. Moreover, once an individual has been successful in his rivalry for a love object with others who desire the same object (such as in cases of love rivalry between suitors, one of whom wins out and marries her), his society generally allows him full expression of any "malignant emotions" engendered by any further efforts to divest him of his "property." In Davis's words, "free expression of malevolent emotion against a trespasser protects the established distribution of property. . . ." The primary "malevolent emotion" that arises as a result of any effort to "trespass" upon one's sexual property is jealousy. "After ownership has been attained, jealousy is a fear and rage reaction fitted to protect, maintain, and prolong the intimate association of love. It shelters this personal relationship from outside intrusion." Thus, according to Davis, most sociocultural systems allow the expression of outrage in situations involving adultery, since "our malignant emotions, fear, anger, hate, and jealousy, greet any illicit attempt to gain property that we hold. . . . The social function of jealousy against a trespasser is the extirpation of any obstacle to the smooth functioning of the institutional machinery." Thus, the basis of the insulting nature of adultery is not in the act itself, but in the fact that in most cultures (though not all), adultery "signifies a violation of accustomed sexual rights." Moreover, the act of adultery in most cultures is not only an insult against the particular individual who is cuckolded, but also, by extension, against the sociocultural system, which has established certain institutions, such as marriage, aimed at defining and maintaining property rights, including "sexual property." Using Davis's analysis, it is possible to understand why the act of adultery in Eskimo culture does not give rise to jealousy: by offering his wife to a guest, the Eskimo husband is emphasizing his ownership of his wife as sexual property, which, as a good host, he desires to share with his guest. Thus, as Davis emphasizes, it is not the act of adultery which is insulting, but rather the fact that in most cultures, with the exception of that of the Eskimos, adultery is a type of "trespass" similar to robbery of material property [Davis, 1936:396–403].

Adultery can thus lead to a strong response against an offender. Among the Murngin tribe of northern Australia, for example, fights are very frequent and are usually the result of quarrels caused by adultery or a husband's belief that someone has been attempting to make him a cuckold. The response of the husband to an offender follows a pattern: carrying a bundle of spears and perhaps a club, he goes to the camp of the lover and accuses him. Words follow, mutual curses are flung, and anger is aroused on both sides. Usually, however, this does not lead to overt violence, since the friends and acquaintances of both men are present and always restrain them from attacking one another. Both opponents make a big display of their anger and, by struggling to get away, show that they are willing to stand up for their rights and to respond violently to insult, even if no actual violence takes place. Thus, both the cuckold and the offender are able to use the threat of violence as a response to insult, but they also depend upon their friends and other bystanders to spare them from actual fighting [Warner, 1937:81].

The possibilities of responding violently to being cuckolded vary substantially in relation to the legal norms of different societies. In some cultures, violence against an adulterer is supported by public opinion and by a legal system which regards the murder of the offender by the cuckolded husband as the proper response. Among the Ifugao tribesmen of the Philippines, for example, an adulterer is sometimes punished by death when taken *in delicto* by the offended spouse, whose revenge is justified by public opinion to a much greater degree than the laws of the United States would condone [Barton, 1919:91].

The legal systems of some societies provide the offended spouse with an effective means of responding to the insult of adultery without having to resort to violence. Moreover, the sense of satisfaction provided by the legal modes of retribution is in most cases enough to prevent violence. The Truk Islanders, for example, provide a legal method for responding to adultery that has proved an effective alternative to violence. Among the Trukese, accusations of adultery lead to a public hearing, and, if those charged are found guilty, they are sentenced to a term in the calaboose. This is evidently an efficient deterrent to violence, as there is little desire to fight on the part of the offended spouses. Hence, the Truk legal system provides a means whereby honor can be satisfied without the risk and anxiety of open physical aggression [Gladwin and Sarason, 1953:241].

Other societies do not provide a definite legal framework through which offended spouses can gain satisfaction. As we have seen in the case of the Murngin, informal norms of restraint serve to prevent overt violence.

In other cultures, violence may not be an acceptable mode of response, but the use of counterinsult may have an even more devastating effect upon an offender than direct violence. An interesting example of revenge against an offender occurred in Manchuria, where it is customary to react to adultery by saying that the offender is "like an animal." Such an insult, while not very serious in our society, is very grave to the Manchu. In one instance recorded by ethnographer Shirokogorov, a man who was absent from home returned early in the morning and found his wife in bed with another man. The husband responded by putting some oats and hay beside the bed to show that the adulterer was like an animal. When the offender awakened he saw the oats and hay and understood their significance. This was so humiliating to him that he hanged himself [Shirokogorov, 1924:152]. Here again we have an example of the centrality of differential cultural meanings: the same kind of counterinsult response would hardly have had such a devastating effect upon an offender if it had occurred in the United States.

Aside from involving merely the adulterer and the cuckold, responses to the insult of adultery may, in some societies, involve the entire community. This is particularly common in tribal and village-based societies characterized by a strong emphasis on kinship ties. In such contexts, any insult directed against an individual, particularly one which undermines the sexual mores and hence the kinship system, is regarded as an offense not only against the individual but against his or her entire family. Thus, in cases of adultery, an entire tribal or village community can get into an uproar. Patterns of response to the insult of adultery can thus often involve entire kin groups rather than particular individuals. Among the Wogeo of Indonesia, for example, adultery is always regarded as an insult against the offended person's clan. This "collectivization" of insult is directly related to the central importance of kinship obligations in the Wogeo culture. Usually, violence is not undertaken against the offender; rather, he is publicly cursed and insulted. And although the resentment that the adulterer feels when he is insulted makes him wish to strike back, he is not able to do so because his own kinsmen will not back him up if they know that he is guilty of the offense. Thus, the adulterer can only listen in silence during his public humiliation; the loss of self-esteem that he suffers is considered an effective punishment for his offense and adequate satisfaction for the insult against the offended man's kin group [Hogbin, 1938:238].

3

THE FAMILY AND INSULT

One of the central differences between modern industrialized societies and both tribal-village and caste-estate systems is that the extended family is no longer of prime importance in modern societies. In most tribal-village societies the extended family is the central social institution around which the entire sociocultural system revolves. Kinship relations and obligations are paramount, and most societal functioning—economic, political, educational, and others—is based on and takes place within the extended family. Modern industrialized societies, on the other hand, are the result of a process of continued differentiation and specialization; functions that are carried out entirely within the framework of tribal-village kinship groups are, in the modern context, performed by specialized institutions: educational, economic, and many others. Hence, the transition from tribal-village to modern industrialized social systems involves a turning away from the centrality of the extended family. In caste-estate systems, the family is a central institution, but its shape and character tend to reflect and reinforce the hierarchical social order rather than to serve as the root institution from which all other functions derive (as in the tribal-village milieu) or as a more or less functionally ambiguous institution, as in the modern context. Let us examine the way in which patterns of insult behavior in each type of family system might help to illuminate the basic differences between them.

Collectivization of Insult in Kinship-Centered Societies

Insult may be regarded as a particular type of negative response which denies the validity of the positive self-image held by an individual or group. In kin-centered tribal and village societies, insults may be directed against an individual, but because of the central importance of his identity as a member of a kin group, the insult is taken as a derogation of the individual's entire family. This collectivization of insult in many tribal villages is an important clue to the way in which such societies view the individual. In modern industrialized societies, with the exception of those with a collectivist ideology, the individual is the basic social unit. In situations involving insult, it is thus the individual's self-regard and reputation that is threatened. In many tribal-village societies, on the other hand, the individual per se has little or no identity outside of his kin group affiliation. Thus, any insult against a member of a kin group is regarded as an affront to the entire group; moreover, responding to an insult is not merely the duty of the particular individual who was the direct object of the insult, but of the entire family. Among the Murngin, for example, the use of obscenity and profanity against a man reflects negatively not only on the man but on his clan. For this reason, obscene insults among individual Murngin almost always result in a fight among the entire membership of the clans involved [Warner, 1937:161].

The norm that defines an insult to an individual as a derogation of his entire kin group is closely related to the strong value such tribal-village cultures place upon a strong sense of family honor and kin group pride. Because family-related insults tend to undermine the centrally important positive self-regard of a kin group, such insults are usually greeted with a strong, collective response from the offended family. In traditional Oriental village cultures, family pride was and in many instances remains centered around reverence for ancestors. Hence, even the slightest derogation of another family's ancestors is considered a grave insult that can easily lead to feuding. In traditional Vietnamese villages, for example, the direst insult is to utter with contempt all the names of another's ancestors. This is far worse than any other insult and can never be forgiven [Vassal, 1910:112]. In prerevolutionary Chinese villages, insult to a family's or clan's ancestors, such as speaking of an ancestor's less worthy deeds, making derisive signs or gestures at an ancestral hall, or damaging an ancestor's grave, caused serious ill feeling between families or clans, whose members learn from their earliest years to defend vigorously their ancestors and all that pertains to them [Yang, 1945:164].

A good example of the way in which a kin-group-centered village culture socializes its children to think of themselves in terms of their families is found in Ammar's account of the social organization of the Fellahin, a traditional Arab subculture, where a child is likely to be praised and positively reinforced for culturally proper behavior not so much as an individual, but in terms of his family. A common statement of praise among the Fellahin is: "You are the son of people who are like princes!" Such praise, which is related to the child's family rather than to the good qualities of the child himself, socializes the child to identify with and submerge himself into the family. Such early family identification leads to a strong sense of family pride among children, who, like adults, often wrangle and quarrel among themselves about the relative status of their families in the community. The following conversation is typical of children's family-related altercations:

"My father is better than yours. He never worked for someone else, and his turban has always been white. My people are all leaders."

"All your people are liars and deceivers," the other boy retorted. "We offer a larger tray of food for guests and on funeral occasions than yours. Your cow is rotting and its bones are sticking out from starvation."

Such insult banter not only helps socialize Fellahin children into the kin-centered attitudes of their culture, but also functions to help define and maintain the patterns of social status among the kin groups that comprise the major units of the social order. In this way, insult behavior is directly related to the establishment and maintenance of the social system of the Fellahin [Ammar, 1954:133].

The emphasis that many tribal-village societies place upon family pride is related to the cultural norm for members of such societies to be extremely touchy about any comments concerning their family or ancestors, no matter how seemingly innocuous. In modern societies, few people would consider it insulting to merely mention or refer to another's ancestors. As Margaret Mead has pointed out, however, the Manus of Samoa consider it a grave insult to recite the genealogy of another's family. The traditional attitude is that one recites the family history of another in order to point out some flaw in it—any reference to another's ancestors can only be an attempt to dishonor them [Mead, 1930:135].

If the mere mention of ancestors is insulting, derogatory comments about one's living relatives are considered in many tribal-village societies to be the worst insults imaginable and therefore call for strong retaliation. Among the Kikuyu, a tribal culture of Kenya, the worst thing that a man can do to infuriate another is to dare to mention his mother's name in an indecent way. This always results in a fight to defend the mother's sacred honor [Kenyatta, 1953:10]. This is not far different from more modern social patterns; in many modern nuclear families, the mother is still a fairly central figure, and in our society insults against her are not usually taken lightly. In general, however, parents and elders are held in much higher esteem in tribal-village societies.

In many tribal-village societies family roles constitute a patterned hierarchy that resembles the familiar "pecking order" of dominance among groups of animals. In most cases, the hierarchy is based on age. Among the Bali of the South Pacific, for example, it is proper for a member of a family to insult, order about, or humiliate a younger member, but not an elder. This system works smoothly, for if one is humiliated by an elder, he may displace his anger on a younger member of the family [Belo, 1936:130].

Among many peoples, there are strong punishments for insulting one's elders, particularly one's parents. In the Ngonde tribe of Africa, a man who insults and fights with his father becomes the object of condemnation by the entire community. Whether the son was in the right is of no consequence; he is regarded as having committed the ultimate wickedness. The chief is informed of the misdeed, and the entire district is informed of the evil thing that has been done. There is no formal denunciation or spoken curse, but it is understood that the "curse of all fathers" and of all ancestors is upon the son. The power of suggestion is very potent in such cases, as the offending son becomes lame and is unable to stand upright. Finally, he becomes a helpless object, crawling around on his buttocks. Thus, even though no direct violent retaliation was suffered by the offender, the effect of community opinion against one who has insulted his parent is so strong that it creates effects more severe than might ensue from a more overt physical response to the offense.

In addition to maintaining the age-based status patterns of many tribal family and kinship systems, prohibitions against insulting elders also function in many societies to protect older people against the neglect and humiliation that their relative lack of usefulness could easily cause them to be subjected to. Often, younger members of a tribal group have second thoughts about offending old people because of the latter's supposed supernatural powers of retaliation. Among the Ngonde, it is considered a severe insult to an old person to remind him even indirectly of his advanced age. In our culture, acts or remarks that would at most be considered tactless are deemed severely insulting in Ngonde. To invite an old man to climb a tree may seem to us more laughable than deadly, but to the Ngonde it is a dreadful insult. Generally, to ask an old person to do anything which is unnatural for him to do is gravely insulting. Even little girls who quite innocently remove their clothes in the presence of an old man are considered to have unwittingly insulted him by reminding him that his time of sexual activity has ended [MacKenzie, 1925:247–49].

The severely insulting character of even the most apparently innocent remark aimed at an elderly Ngonde may be related to the fact that in the Ngonde and similar tribal societies there are no means other than strong prohibition to protect older persons from insult-related abuse and neglect. In many tribal-village contexts, the threat of supernatural retaliation is virtually the only way to insure that older people will be granted the necessities of survival. Among the Azande, for example, it is considered severely insulting to old people to fail to give them a share of the food that is available. The culturally defined supernatural power, or Mangu, of the elderly is used as a threat to make sure that the younger members of an Azande family do not forget their responsibilities to their elders. An Azande who kills an animal must make sure that he sends presents of the meat to all the old men and women who live near him. If an old person receives no meat or beer he or she will prevent, with supernatural abilities, any more animals from being killed [Evans-Pritchard, 1929:112]. Among the Saulteaux Indians of North America, children are cautioned at an early age not to laugh at or ridicule old people. No abstract ethical ideal is involved; it is simply a matter of defense against the supposed supernatural power of the elderly [Hallowell, 1955:284].

In tribal-village societies, then, patterns of insult prohibition serve to sustain the age-based stratification system. Parents and old persons are venerated, and insults against them are treated as severe transgressions of the moral order. Can the same pattern be found in caste-estate societies?

Patriarchy and Insult in the Caste-Estate Context

The family patterns of most caste-estate societies are a microcosm of the rigidly hierarchical sociocultural macrocosm. Caste-estate societies are most clearly distinguished by their emphasis upon the innate superiority and inferiority, respectively, of their upper and lower social strata. Just as people are sharply differentiated from one another on the basis of their social position and, by cosmic extension, of their supposed rank in the hierarchy of creation, the members of caste-estate families occupy positions in a clearly graded hierarchy, the most notable features of which are the overweening prestige, power, and inviolability of the father. In caste-estate systems, however, it is not the age of the father so much as his masculine identity that provides the basis of his high status. Thus, caste-estate families are essentially patriarchal subsystems in which females of nearly any age have decidedly inferior status to males.

Insult plays a definite role in maintaining the male-dominated patterns of patriarchal families. In many caste-estate societies, women are treated with contempt and are continually reminded of their inferior status. Humiliations and insults begin at a very early age, if indeed the girl is lucky enough to survive infancy. The birth of a girl is anything but a joyful event; in India, it is a definite disappointment. Having been born a female is considered by the Hindu religious perspective to be a punishment for sins committed in a previous incarnation. When a Hindu man learns that he has become the father of a girl, he may well announce to his friends that "nothing" has happened. The friends then depart, gravely and quietly. In many instances female infants are deliberately neglected and often allowed to die. In extreme, though by no means uncommon cases in China and India, female infants were deliberately put to death.

Far from prohibiting brutal treatment of girls and women, the religions of traditional caste-estate societies serve in part to define and sustain the inferiority of women, and to define their role within the family as one of complete submission and obedience. Throughout the sacred religious writings of many caste-estate cultures are many insulting comments about women, as well as prohibitions which make it a grave sin for a woman even to think of responding to an insult that might be directed against her by a male member of her family. In the Manu, a set of Hindu sacred writings, for example, it is stated that "a woman . . . should endure without anger or indignation the jeers of others, suffering such things with patience and humility." Above all, the woman occupies a secondary and inferior status within the family: "A woman must look to her husband as her lord, and must serve him with all worship and reverence. The great lifelong duty of a woman is obedience. When the husband issues his instructions, the wife must never disobey them. . . . She should look on her husband as if he were Heaven itself" [quoted in Mace and Mace, 1960:69–71].

The patriarchal system further insults and humiliates women by a vicious circle effect: women in caste-estate societies are deliberately kept uneducated and are prevented from leaving their homes, and then are berated by men for their stupidity and narrow-mindedness. A typical Hindu Brahmin attitude is expressed in this insult against women: "Educate a woman and you put a knife into the hands of a monkey" [Hauswirth, 1930:147].

Such insulting attitudes toward women, which serve to keep them in a subordinate position within the male-dominated family, are by no means found only in India. The use of insult has in the past been—and in many cultures remains—an important means of subjugating women to a narrowly circumscribed role of little or no power within the family. In medieval Europe, insults against women were part and parcel of Christian theology, which laid the groundwork for many of the attitudes which are still very influential today. Just as the Indian woman was considered to be on a lower level of being than her husband, the patriarchal family structure of European civilization was a microcosmic reflection of the aristocratic class hierarchy that provided the basis of the medieval social order. Moreover, the dualistic Christian worldview (which bifurcated both the natural and the unseen realms into Good and Evil, God and the Devil, and so forth) was reflected in insulting definitions of women set forth by prominent theologians. St. Thomas Aquinas, for example, provided a theological justification for the subjugation of women by stressing the supposed innate incapacity of women to be anything but a family functionary. He speaks of woman as a necessary object who is needed to preserve the species or to provide food and drink. Woman was created to be man's helpmate. In extreme forms, theological insults against women took the form of a direct identification of women as the embodiment of sin. According to St. Jerome, "Woman is the gate of the devil, the path of wickedness, the sting of the serpent, in a word a perilous object" [Bullough, 1973:232; 234].

Have such attitudes persisted in our present time? How is insult used within the modern family? Let us turn now to an examination of the various functions that insult behavior serves as one means whereby the patterns of modern family life are defined and maintained.

Insult and Togetherness: Nagging as the Great Equalizer

Though we have no data to prove such an assertion, it seems likely that most insults within caste and traditional families were directed by husbands against wives, as a tool to insure the continuation of women's subjugation. As present-day women's liberation efforts have so forcefully pointed out, women are still the object of insults not only from their husbands, but also from society at large, which tends to relegate them to a subordinate role and to deny them options other than those related to the maintenance of the family. Within the modern family, however, it seems likely that insult is no longer quite as unidirectional: it appears that modern women may use insult as one of the few means available to them of exercising power over their husbands.

The modern family differs from its primitive, caste, and traditional counterparts by the existence of a belief system which at least gives lip service to the idea that man and wife should be equal "partners." Ideally, the modern family should be a democracy in which the husband and wife make decisions together. Since differing attitudes can never lead to a majority in a dyad, and since children's attitudes are often not seriously considered, the egalitarian ideal of the man-wife partnership rarely works out well in practice. Inevitably, situations arise in which there are conflicting opinions, and a power struggle ensues. In such a situation, the husband holds most of the trump cards. Assuming the typicality of the relationship, it is his job, his occupational prestige, that provides the basis of the family's social standing as well as its financial resources. Thus, even though she might be ambitious, the now working wife has little power to determine her own social mobility; any "social climbing" on her part necessarily depends upon the social acceptability of her husband's standing in the community. In a deeper sense, this means that the wife's basic sense of meaning and purpose in life is tied to her husband's potentialities, since it is his success which will determine her own destiny as well as her children's. In such a situation, the wife becomes acutely sensitized to her husband's shortcomings, since it is these which could undermine her chances to fulfill her own ambitions. By pointing out these shortcomings to him by nagging and by subtle and not-so-subtle insults, she is able to exercise some degree of power over him and hence alleviate her complete subjugation to him while at the same time giving vent to her frustrations.

To be sure, much of the insult that takes place between husband and wife is of the variety that we will discuss in our examination of insults and primary group relations—it consists of good-natured teasing and "kidding." In many marriages, however, insults serve the non-"kidding" functions of power assertion and alleviation of frustration. Surprisingly enough, there is a relative dearth of sociological research dealing with this important topic. In lieu of scholarly references, let us examine one of the most successful and well-known dramatic studies of insult between marriage partners, Edward Albee's *Who's Afraid of Virginia Woolf?*

One reason for the success of this play is that it exposes the manner in which blatant insults are employed by a modern wife in order to give vent to her frustrations and gain some measure of alleviation of her feeling that her marriage has entailed an abrogation of her personal ambitions, as well as leaving her powerless to do anything about her own destiny. Albee's play is a perfect illustration of the manner in which the modern wife's thwarted hopes of social mobility and "success," not matched by the ambition or capacities of her husband, give rise to a veritable orgy of insult and vituperation against them. Throughout the play, the husband is continually bombarded with insults, nearly all of which refer to his inability to "succeed" in conventional terms: to move up the academic hierarchy, to become the dean of his college. But the particular setting is not important; the husband could as well be a businessman or some other type of professional:

Martha: I had it all planned out . . . He'd take over some day . . . That was the way it was supposed to be . . . Daddy seemed to think it was a pretty good idea, too. For a while . . . Until he watched for a couple of years and started thinking that maybe Georgie-boy didn't have the stuff . . . that he didn't have it in him!
George: Stop it, Martha!
Martha: (Viciously triumphant)—The hell I will! You see, George didn't have much . . . push . . . he wasn't particularly . . . aggressive. In fact he was sort of a . . . (Spits the word at George's aback) . . . a FLOP! a great . . . big . . . fat . . . FLOP!
George: (Almost crying)—I said stop, Martha.
Martha: So here I am, stuck with this flop . . . this BOG in the History Department.

George: . . . don't, Martha, don't . . .

Martha: . . . who's married to the President's daughter, who's expected to be somebody, not just some nobody, some bookworm, somebody who's so damn . . . contemplative, he can't make anything out of himself, somebody without the guts to make anybody proud of him . . ."

As the content of Martha's diatribes shows, modern society's mobility and "success" values intrude upon and may well undermine family cohesion. In most primitive and traditional contexts, in contrast, strong norms of response to family-related insults strengthen family solidarity. Our comparative examination of insult behavior thus underscores the centrality of the extended family in many primitive and traditional contexts, and its diminished importance as a core institution in modern societies.

4

SOCIAL STRATIFICATION
AND INSULT

Social stratification refers to the forms and functions of patterns of social inequality. Every society has some form of ranking which constitutes a means of either assigning or allowing individuals comprising the society a greater or lesser degree of the rewards that the system has to offer. Unequal distribution of rewards occurs along several dimensions. When the rewards are primarily tangible, we speak of economic stratification; rewards that are essentially normative, such as prestige and honor, constitute the basis of social status. In many societies, the two go together; a highly disproportionate share of tangible rewards is often, though not always, closely associated with high social status.

Insult as a Legitimation of Social Inequality

Insult is one means by which social stratification systems are both constituted and maintained. Since every society has individuals and subgroups who receive either more or less than their proportionate share of its wealth, rewards, and privileges, the dominant group, in order to maintain its position, must somehow justify its privileges. Such justification is usually accomplished, in most societies, in two closely related ways: first, by the dominant group's assertion that its privileges are warranted because of innately superior abilities and achievements; and second, by a contention that those who are lower in the status order are either innately inferior or do not work hard enough. When an elite's derogation of the abilities or achievements of a lower-status group becomes overt, we have a type of patterned insult behavior which, through ritualized acts or repeated statements, serves both to justify and sustain a society's pattern of social stratification.

Response to insult is often just as important as a means of maintaining the stratification systems of a certain society. There are often differential norms governing response to insults by members of higher and lower social strata. Because high prestige and high status depend upon a definition of the highly placed individual or subgroup as a superior social object, any insult directed against a high-status individual is not only directed against him as a particular person, but also by implication against the entire sociocultural order which accords to him and justifies his high position. In other words, to attack a highly placed individual or subgroup of a society through insult means that the insulter is by extension undermining the entire sociocultural system from which the social hierarchy derives the legitimation of its values and normative system. Hence, in nearly every kind of society there are stronger norms against insulting personages more highly placed than lower-status individuals or groups. Indeed, as we shall emphasize, semiritualized insulting of low-status elements is often encouraged because it functions to maintain the society's defintion of the innate inferiority of the lowly placed and the socially disadvantaged. Hence, insult can serve to maintain a society's stratification system because it reaffirms the justification of unequally distributed rewards and privileges. Let us see how this status-related function of insult behavior is evident in each of our three basic kinds of social orders.

Insult and Status in Tribal and Village Societies

Because of the relatively small-scale character of most tribal and village societies, their systems of social stratification are relatively less formalized than those of caste-estate and modern societies. In other words, tribal and village cultures definitely exhibit established patterns of social inequality, but these patterns tend to be somewhat less complex and less formally institutionalized than in more "advanced" societies. A prime reason for this is the fact that the comparatively small size of tribal-village societies allows everyone to be known as an individual and as a member of a particular family. This close contact between village inhabitants or tribal members makes it difficult both for norms of social distance and patterns of social segregation of higher and lower status subgroups to develop and be maintained.

For these reasons, stratification among the members of a tribe, or fellow villagers, is often "emergent"; i.e., it is not necessarily based on long-established, inherited patterns of privilege and power but must be continually established, reestablished, and affirmed, as is generally true in any small group in which individuals are in daily and continual face-to-face interaction. Insult is an important means by which individuals or subgroups in a tribal-village society assert their superior status by denigrating other individuals. A good example is provided in an account of a tragic incident among the members of a Jordanian village, in which a woman's assertion of her and her family's claim to social superiority led to a strong and violent reaction from those she had insulted:

"I have the greatest honor in this village!" the woman had boasted.
"No, by the name of the Prophet, I have the greatest honor in the village! . . . See what a great man my husband is . . . And look at the jackal face of this Ahmad of yours."
In a moment stones were thrown and everybody was shouting abuse [McCown, 1922:787].

In an ensuing melee, a child was hit by a rock and killed. In spite of this tragedy, the patterns of insult and counterinsult served as one means of either reaffirming or reestablishing the relative statuses of the families involved. In similar instances, particularly when insult leads to protracted violence, insult behavior can serve as the basis of feuds between individuals and families. Feuds stemming from status competition and related insult and counterinsult are more likely to occur in tribal and village cultures than in caste-estate or modern societies because of the previously mentioned lack, in tribal and village societies, of a formalized, institutionalized system of stratification in which there is comparatively less ambiguity concerning the relative status of families and individuals.

Although the various families comprising a tribe or village are not as clearly differentiated from one another in terms of their status as are families in caste-estate or modern societies, the high status accorded the chief of the tribe does involve strong norms proscribing insult against the chief. Although there are relatively few such formal positions of high status, the prestige of those who do occupy them is protected by norms that define any derogatory remarks against a chieftain, no matter how seemingly innocuous, as serious insults. The same remarks directed at persons of lesser social standing are not considered insults. This means that the status-formalization that does exist in tribal and village cultures serves for the most part to sustain the prestige of the headman. In the tribal society of the Maori, for example, particularly at times of feasting, there is a strict etiquette that must be followed in order to make sure that proper respect and deference are paid to the individual of highest status. Any breach of such etiquette would be considered a grave insult to the chief. The chieftain has to be served first at the tribal feasts, and Maori norms specify that he is to receive a portion commensurate with his high station. If a tribal subordinate would deliberately serve himself first or take a larger portion than the chief, the latter would consider it a grave insult. Thus, the Maori, similar to many tribal societies, place a strong emphasis upon the honor of the chief. Any remark or act directed against a chief is easily interpreted as an insult, to which the chief is likely to respond violently so as to protect and maintain his high prestige. Moreover, the high prestige of the Maori chiefs is liable to render them much more touchy than the average member of the tribe. As Firth points out, the pride that a Maori chief takes in his high position is liable to make him an exceedingly sensitive person who is quick to resent any act that he regards as a denigration and therefore a threat to his prestige. The readiness of Maori chiefs to define innocent acts or remarks as insulting has led to a great deal of quarreling and fighting within the tribe. The reaction of a chief to a perceived insult is strong and usually violent primarily because any derogation is directed not only against the chief as an individual, but against the prestige and honor of his position, which in turn represents and symbolizes the honor of the entire tribe. Thus, rather than being a mere personal idiosyncrasy, as a nonsociological analysis might assume, the excessive touchiness of tribal chiefs is a phenomenon which can be explained in terms of the prestige of the chief's high position and the collective tribal honor symbolized by that position [Firth, 1959:325].

In one instance, a seemingly innocent remark was interpreted by a Maori chief as a grave insult. The high Maori chief Kahukura was walking along a beach one day. Just offshore a man in a boat had caught a small fish which was red in color. The fisherman held up his catch and said in a laughing manner to his companions in the boat, "That man on the beach is like this fish," referring to Kahukura, who was daubed with red ochre as part of his ceremonial dress. The chief, overhearing this remark, took great offense at being compared with a fish and considered the remark a grave insult. The next morning, Kahukura's warriors attacked and destroyed the offender's village [Buck, 1952:387–88].

Kahukura's violent response to the fisherman's insult was relatively unstructured and spontaneous in that it did not involve any formal, institutionalized ritual of seeking revenge for the insult. Nonetheless, it was doubtlessly effective as a means of maintaining his prestige. In traditional caste and estate societies, individuals occupying high position, particularly members of the aristocracy, exhibit similar degrees both of sensitivity to insult and of willingness to respond violently to any act or remark that is the least disparaging of their honor. The substantial differences between the tribal and the caste and estate patterns lie first of all in the fact that the latter systems define not just the chief but the entire aristocratic class as socially honorable. And second, the caste and estate systems tend to provide elaborate, institutionalized means of responding to perceived insult. Thus, the aristocrats of an estate or caste system are just as touchy as tribal and village chiefs, but they are less likely to respond to an insult with unstructured, spontaneous violence because their cultures provide patterned, formalized means of responding to insults. In addition, most caste and estate systems minimize the possibility that a lower-status person will insult a member of the aristocracy by providing elaborate, systematic norms of social distance which segregate the higher class from their inferiors on the social hierarchy. In the Indian caste system, a highly ritualized form of insult and humiliation against the lower-order elements, the Untouchables, continually underscores the socially defined innate superiority of the highest-order Brahmins and hence functions to minimize the possibility that insults might be directed against Brahmins by the members of the lower castes, particularly Untouchables. The Indian caste system is similar to the tribal village social order in that it attaches high honor and prestige to its highest social stratum. The caste system differs, however, in the manner in which it uses insult to maintain the honor and prestige of the Brahmins. Rather than allowing the Brahmins to wreak revenge upon those who have insulted their caste, the system provides elaborate norms of social avoidance and social distance so as, in part, to make social situations in which insults might be exchanged relatively rare and hence to protect them against insults that could undermine their prestige and honor as Brahmins. At this point, let us examine the caste system's use of insult and insult-avoidance as a mechanism for maintaining India's rigidly hierarchical pattern of social stratification.

Insult and the Maintenance of the Indian Caste Order

Just as the tribal or village chief comes to regard himself as superior by virtue of his high position, thus the Brahmin from his earliest years is socialized to view himself as innately superior to the lower castes, particularly the Untouchables. The Indian caste system, according to an excellent analysis by the French sociologist Dumont, is based upon the concept of purity. In order to sustain this central cultural value, it is essential for the Indian sociocultural system to provide means whereby the purity of the Brahmins might not be defiled through contact with Untouchables, since such contact and consequent defilement could threaten and undermine the foundations upon which the Indian caste order is based. Thus the society provides a set of elaborate norms of social distance, particularly between Brahmins and Untouchables. A basic element of this system of norms is the sense of superiority that the Brahmin internalizes as part of his caste-related socialization. And this sense of innate superiority is inseparable from a corresponding contempt for all those who are of lower caste, particularly Untouchables. This contempt is reinforced by various kinds of ritualized humiliations and insults that Untouchables are obliged to undergo as part of the norms of avoidance and social distance that are aimed at maintaining the cultural definition of Untouchables as inherently inferior and impure.

The Brahmin is brought up from his earliest youth to think of non-Brahmins as infinitely beneath him, and he looks upon those of lower caste as having been created solely to serve him and to minister to his needs. Correspondingly, he considers it a kind of duty to his own caste to treat non-Brahmins, particularly Untouchables, with hatred, contempt, and harshness. The cultural basis for the Brahmin's sense of superiority and his related practice of incivility toward the members of lower castes rests ultimately upon the Hindu worldview, which serves as the underlying set of taken-for-granted assumptions concerning the universal order of reality and man's place in the universe. According to the Indian world-view, the universe as a whole, including mankind, is a hierarchy the levels of which are related to the degrees of purity of the different layers of existence. Thus, the Indian worldview divides society into ranks depending upon the supposed degrees of purity of each social level. In the caste system, which is the earthly-societal manifestation of the cosmic hierarchy, the lower castes, particularly the Untouchables, constitute a lower level of being than the Brahmins. So the Untouchables are regarded, and treated, as being something less than fully human. Institutionalized patterns of humiliation and insult are one means of maintaining such cultural definitions, as well as social distance and social separation between the Brahmins and the Untouchables. By virtue of their socialization as outcasts, Untouchables internalize the cultural definition of their supposed innate inferiority and learn to conform to these ritualized patterns of avoidance of Brahmins and to maintain their humble Untouchable status. Thus, the socialization process of the Untouchables in effect teaches and requires them to participate actively in their own collective self-abnegation and degradation [Dubois, 1906:315]. As we shall see in our examination of minority-group socialization and insult, this pattern of the participation of the insulted in their own denigration is by no means restricted to the Indian caste system.

Examples of the manner in which Untouchables perpetuate their own collective self-denigration through active participation in rituals of insult and avoidance can be found in many scholarly studies of the caste system. Hutton points out that in some parts of India, Untouchables were required to use special, degrading language when referring to themselves, their families, or their possessions [Hutton, 1951:86; 125-26]. To underscore their culturally defined lack of full status as human beings, Untouchables were obliged to call their children "calves" or some other term denoting young animals. When addressing Brahmins, Untouchables never used the first-person pronoun "I" to refer to themselves, but rather were required to say something like "Your humble dog respectfully requests." In any interaction between an Untouchable and a Brahmin, the Untouchable was thus required to refer continually to and reemphasize his own supposedly subhuman status. There were in some parts of India many ritual humilia-tions which the Untouchable was required to perform whenever in physical proximity to Brahmins. These rituals were all designed to prevent the defilement of Brahmins, who were the embodiments of culturally defined purity. In some parts of southern India, until quite recent times, Untouchables were required to prostrate themselves on the ground during the day whenever a Brahmin was close by, so that the "impure" shadows of the Untouchables might not fall upon a holy Brahmin. Similarly, Untouchables often had to carry branches after themselves in order to erase their footprints, which a Brahmin might chance to walk over and hence become defiled. Needless to say, Brahmins tried to keep as much physical distance as possible between themselves and Untouchables, lest their Brahmin purity be in danger of defilement. Each morning, Brahmins underwent elaborate purification rituals, which would have to be repeated vigorously in case of contact, however slight, with Untouchables during the course of the day. The lengths to which the Brahmin fear of defilement could go is illustrated by an ethnographer's account of two small Brahmin girls, who, after merely having looked at an Untouchable, ran home and washed out their eyes with soap [Ghurye, 1950:9–12].

Is this type of ritual participation by the lower class in its own humiliation found only in India? Many scholars have pointed out that the American South may be regarded as a type of caste system in which blacks have been and continue to be treated in ways similar to the patterns of insult and humiliation inflicted upon Indian Untouchables. For example, the underlying value of purity and its opposite, impurity, is evinced in the Southern white culture's emphasis upon norms of avoidance aimed at preventing defiling contact with blacks at water fountains, public toilets, on buses, and in other places. Although the manifest function of the traditional Southern laws is social segregation, an important latent function is found in the assumption that the purity of the white race, basically similar to the purity of the Indian Brahmin, must not be defiled. Another similarity between the Indian and the Southern uses of insult to maintain the status order is found in the norms of address: just as the Indian Untouchables had to refer to themselves and their relatives using animal referents, Southern whites often refer to blacks as "monkeys," and through various other kinds of insult and humiliation, attempt to deny the full humanity of blacks. Thus, the general patterns of insult usage in the Indian and the Southern American caste systems are basically similar. Such use of insult is, moreover, by no means confined solely to caste systems. In modern industrial societies, as we shall examine in detail later in this chapter, the low status of minority groups is in part maintained by a pattern of semiritualized collective insults that serve to reemphasize and sustain the cultural definition of minority group members as inherently inferior. At this point, let us turn to an examination of another type of society, the estate system, to examine the ways in which insult and response to insult help maintain the hierarchical system of social stratification, particularly in regard to the society's provision for response to insult among members of the land-owning aristocracy.

Duelling and the Maintenance of Aristocratic Honor

The estate system is similar to the caste type of social order in that both kinds of societies are based upon a strongly hierarchical system of social inequality which emphasizes the superiority of the upper class and the culturally defined inferiority of the lower classes. The basic difference is that the economic power and prestige of the estate aristocracy is based upon the ownership of land and control over the military. In the pure caste society, as in India, the Brahmins do not constitute a military elite, nor do they directly involve themselves in economic pursuits. In addition, the estate system is somewhat more fluid than the caste order since the priestly estate provides a means of upward mobility. In the caste system, the Brahmins constitute the religious elite, to which they and no other caste can belong.

Since the prestige and dominant social status of an estate aristocracy depends in part upon its position as the military elite, the male members of the aristocracy are socialized from their earliest youth in the values and means of warfare and formalized violence. In addition, just as Brahmins internalize a sense of their caste-related innate superiority, aristocrats in the estate society are imbued with values that emphasize their prestige as members of the upper class and their obligation to defend their honor, not only as individuals but as representatives of the highest class. In certain traditional societies, notably Prussian Germany and the antebellum South, duelling was the prescribed means by which the aristocratic gentleman defended his honor. Let us examine the institution of duelling not only for what it can tell us about formalized, violent means of response to insult, but for the light it might shed upon the nature of the sociocultural order in which it was found.

As a means of redressing grievances and responding to insult, the duel has virtually disappeared except in isolated instances in South America. A nonlethal form of duelling persists in some fraternities in German universities, however. This survival-form of duelling involves heavily masked youths who attempt to inflict wounds on one another's cheeks. The resulting gash, or "Schmiss," is a highly valued symbol of the fraternity man's upper-class status as well as his manly courage. The kind of duel we are about to examine was much more deadly than that of contemporary German fraternities. It flourished throughout the eighteenth and nineteenth centuries in three particular Western milieux: Prussia, the antebellum South, and post-Napoleonic France. Because of our lack of data on French duelling, and because it generally was less lethal than duelling in Prussia or in America (in France, swords were used, and the duel was terminated at the first drawing of blood), we shall limit out discussion to the Prussian and American versions.

In Prussia, officers of the Kaiser's army were expected to defend their honor as aristocrats, and duelling was very frequent in the years preceding World War I. In America, although several duels took place outside the South (notably the famous Hamilton-Burr duel), it was most prevalent in the South, particularly before the Civil War. The fact that both the South and Prussia were caste societies with certain philosophical roots in romanticism and neo-medieval chivalric values suggests the tentative hypothetical relationship between the caste order and the practice of duelling. Specifically, the institution of duelling was an important aspect in the maintenance of an aristocratic upper class that was threatened, in the nineteenth century, by the prevalence of democratic societies and the forces of industrialization. To an aristocracy whose way of life, assumptions of superiority, and chivalric values were increasingly attacked as outmoded and neo-medieval by modern industrialized cultures, the defense of the individual aristocrat's "honor" served to legitimate and defend not only the individual but the very system upon which his sense of honor was based. To draw a theoretical analogy, functional analyses of deviant behavior maintain that the recognition and punishment of deviant behavior may serve positive functions by reaffirming values and normative standards. In his analysis of deviance and punishment in Puritan New England, for example, Erikson maintains that the persecution of Quakers and "witches" took place in a period of various forces of both a social and religious nature, which led many of the Puritans to define any kind of religious nonconformity as not only heretical, but criminal. The Puritans thus used the persecution of Quakers and other nonconformists as one important means of maintaining their social and economic dominance over colonial New England [Erikson, 1966]. Similarly, the high incidence of duelling in the antebellum South and Prussia is related to the latent function of duelling as a means of reaffirming upper-caste values and a neo-feudal chivalric culture. The specific ways in which formalized, violent response helped maintain the caste system and caste values is well illustrated in the culturally prescribed methods for dealing with perceived insult in the Prussian culture. The relationship between the concept of "honor" and the caste system is also relevant. Specifically, "honor" may be viewed as a culturally instilled conception of self as sacred social object; i.e., a social object "higher" in the divinely ordered scale of being. Hence, the defense of one's honor against insult served not only to uphold one's self-esteem and the caste order, but also, implicitly, the divine order of reality. Only when these cultural factors are recognized is it possible to comprehend the functional reasons underlying the vehemence of the Prussian Junker's response to insult, as written by Martin:

The "code of honor" prescribes humiliation of the offender by abuse and violence if he is inferior in class. A duel is required if he is of acceptably high social standing—one of the nobility, an army officer, a student or graduate of a university. The insult or imagined insult is welcomed since it offers the opportunity to defend one's honor and display one's prowess. It is "smart" to fight because it is "smart" to belong to the caste of people who are "*satisfaktionsfaehig*"—entitled to give or receive satisfaction for offense by a duel [Martin, 1945:40].

The Prussian culture thus not only prescribed violence, both formal and spontaneous, as a response to insult, but also afforded a sociocultural context within which acts and remarks were much more likely to be situationally defined as insults.

Norms of the Art of Duelling: The Code Duello

The practice of duelling involved strict etiquette and demanded rigorous adherence to prescribed procedures. Duellists often employed experts in the codes of duelling as advisers on the correctness of their actions both in preparing for the duel, and on the field of honor itself. Witnesses were often brought along to attest that the combatants had followed proper procedures.

The emphasis on correctness of conduct can be exemplified by the fact that several books containing sets of rules were published in the South, one of which had been written by a governor of North Carolina. Among these rules are the following:

Rule 14. Seconds are to be of equal rank in society with the principals they attend, in so much as a second may choose or chance to become a principal and equality is indispensible.

Rule 20. Firing may be regulated, but by signal; secondly, by word of command; or thirdly, at the latter case the parties may fire at their reasonable leisure, but second presents and rests are strictly prohibited.

Article 1. No party can be allowed to cover the knee or cover his side with his left hand; but may present from any level from the hip to the eye [Seitz, 1929:10].

There are many such regulations. One of the main functions of the high degree of formalization appears to be related to the necessity for the gentlemen involved to differentiate their fighting as much as possible from the mere brawling in which only the lower orders engaged. The formalization of duelling thus also functions to maintain the aristocratic assumption of superiority.

There was often an involved and elaborate interaction that took place between principals before they actually arrived at the duelling field. Specifically, an exchange of notes usually took place, the ostensible purpose of which was for the object of a remark or act to inquire as to whether the perpetrator had intended an insult. A typical note read:

I presume that you will state whether you meant any personal disrespect or to intimate that I was deficient in integrity, honor, or any other quality requisite to the character of a gentleman.

Often a lengthy exchange of notes took place, all of which can be regarded as formal attempts by the aggrieved to define the situation as an insult. When the replies either confirmed the supposition of insult, or were pointedly evasive, the result was a formal challenge:

Having failed at all my efforts at an amiable adjustment of the difficulties between us, nothing remains for me but to demand of you the satisfaction usual among gentlemen [Seitz, 1929:44-46].

The definition of an act or a remark as insulting can be regarded as the result of a set of decisions arising out of a particular type of symbolic interaction. The preliminary exchange of notes leading to a formal challenge was, at the same time, subject to substantial cultural influences. In other words, both the manner in which the insult came to be defined as such, and the individual's decision to regard it as such, were not entirely "created" acts of choice: cultural values and definitions heavily influenced both the manner and the determination of the insult. In simple terms, what is regarded as an insult in one culture may be overlooked as wholly inoffensive in another context. A striking example of this is a dispute between two well-known Arkansas judges of the 1820s, one of whom was a transplanted Northerner who was not fully socialized to the stringent norms governing interaction with upper-class women. The two judges were playing cards with two ladies at a fashionable card party. As the game progressed, one of the ladies exclaimed:

"Judge Selden, we have the tricks and honors on you!" Judge Selden blinked. Even the fact that he came from the North did not require him to accept an obvious error. "That is not so," said Judge Selden, quietly. The lady, very much mortified at the ungracious reply, put up her handkerchief to hide her quivering lips, and also her aggrieved ladyhood. Today's reader may wonder where lay the black injury in the Judge's statement of fact: the reader obviously was not in Arkansas in the 1820s [Kane, 1951:211-13].

The other judge at the card table immediately defended the lady's honor by challenging Judge Selden, without the formal preliminaries, to a duel. Several days later Selden was killed on the field of honor. In this example we are reminded of Thomas's statement to the effect that if situations are defined as real, they are real in their consequences. A remark which would be regarded as purely cognitive in one culture is defined as extremely insulting in another, with tragically real consequences for those who fail to conform to the norms reflecting such definitions.

Earlier we mentioned the close connection between insult and humor. This point is particularly salient in one instance where an intended practical joke was taken seriously by its recipient. Two doctors in California, one a former Southerner, had been friends for many years but had some differences of opinion concerning racial matters. The ex-Southerner, in order to give his more liberal friend a "closer" understanding of Negroes, found a corpse of a black child and placed it in his friend's bed. The friend, Wilson, was furious, and his affection for Whiteman, the Southerner, immediately turned to extreme rage as he vowed to "kill Whiteman if it's the last thing I do." They soon met on the field of honor, and the practical joker paid for his fun with his life [Kane, 1951:121].

A similar instance of a lack of congruence in definitions of intended humor can be found in the example offered in a later chapter concerning Andrew Jackson. Jackson failed to see the humor in one of his colleague's practical jokes; however, although he considered challenging the jokester to a duel, he was dissuaded by the strenuous efforts of mutual friends.

Both of these instances of duelling behavior illustrate the saliency not only of cultural prescriptions and definitions of insult, but also of personality variables in the incidence of duelling. One element of personality, in addition to the sense of self which, as we have seen, is directly related in the identity of the "gentleman" to a particular social structure, is the underlying temperament of the individual. The influence of temperament upon duelling behavior is apparent throughout the literature on the practice. Obviously, in the definition of a remark as insulting and in the subsequent challenge, cultural factors alone, while exerting a certain pressure toward defining and challenging the insulter, often were not sufficient to bring about a duel. Both the challenger and the challenged had to have sufficient temperamental aggressiveness in order for the duel actually to take place. In the examples of Judge Selden and Andrew Jackson, we are told that both Selden's challenger and Jackson were men who basically enjoyed a good fight and who were therefore temperamentally predisposed toward engaging in duels. The literature contains a wealth of stories concerning "knightly" gentlemen of the South and Prussian officers who made virtual careers out of successful duelling. On the other hand, there are many examples of men who had a temperamental aversion to duelling. For example, although he was repeatedly challenged, Robert E. Lee managed to avoid entering into duels, in part because of his reputation for courage. Often, however, in spite of a strong temperamental anticlivity for the practice, an aristocratic gentleman was pressured onto the field of honor by social opinion. Perhaps the most noted example of this was Alexander Hamilton's reluctance to accept Aaron Burr's challenge. Even though he finally accompanied Burr to Weehawken, Hamilton maintained what Erving Goffman might term "civil inattention." Prior to the duel, he ignored Burr's challenge as much as possible, and at the scene refused to take a serious attitude toward the duel, firing into the air. Hamilton's somewhat aloof attitude and his attempt to maintain civil inattention evidently served only to strengthen Burr's resolve to carry out his lethal intentions.

In summary, duelling is a practice which has, with very scattered exceptions, died out with the demise of the aristocracies that supported it. Wherever duelling was prevalent—in the American South, in Prussian Junker society, and elsewhere—it was a major means of sustaining the culturally conditioned sense of innate superiority of the men who occupied the uppermost castes. As a mode of response to insult, it was thus instrumental in maintaining and sustaining the aristocratic caste societies of Europe and America.

Insult and Status in Modern Egalitarian Societies

Modern industrialized societies, such as contemporary America, are characterized by an anomaly: on the one hand, the manifest ideologies of most industrialized societies emphasize a belief in egalitarianism—that men are created equal and should have equal opportunities. On the other hand, despite the fact that most people, when asked, will reply that they are "middle class," there are definite gradations of social status and economic reward attached to different occupations and levels of educational attainment. In other words, egalitarian ideology appears at times as mere lip service against the reality of social class. Nonetheless, despite the fact that ideals of equality have not been worked out in practice, their existence has important implications for the way insults are employed to define and maintain social distinctions. In caste societies, as we have seen, insult and humiliation of lower-caste members are used in a blatant manner to continually sustain and reaffirm the culturally defined innate inferiority of the lower castes. Since the world view and ideology of such societies legitimate and support such practices, there is little if any subtlety in their application. But in cultures which give at least lip service to egalitarian values, insults designed to keep the lower classes "in their place" must of necessity be somewhat more subtle and indirect, since insults of the more blatant variety (as against Untouchables) lack the kind of world view and ideological support found in societies with either definite castes or aristocratic upper classes.

Accordingly, insults directed against those of low social or occupational status in American society are often somewhat indirect, but nonetheless humiliating to their recipients. A good example is provided by Ray Gold in his study of the occupational role and attitudes of a janitor [Gold, 1952:491]. Janitors have low prestige in relation to other occupations; the North-Hatt scale of occupational prestige places them close to the bottom, just above garbagemen and shoe-shiners, in terms of the percentage of respondents who consider the janitor's job socially desirable. Janitors, like others of low occupational status, are continually reminded of their position in ways which convey the disdain with which their role is viewed, but in most cases without the kind of blatant, formalized humiliation and insult characteristic of the treatment of menials in caste and aristocratic-class societies. The kind of status-related insults that janitors are subjected to are well illustrated in Gold's interviews with a number of janitors working in apartment buildings:

Interviewer: What things are janitors touchy about?
Janitor: A lot of tenants figure he's just . . . a servant. They put on airs and try to be bossy. You say something to them and they . . . say, "Hell, you're nothing but a janitor." Or when you're talking to even a working man and you tell him you're a janitor, he smiles—you know, people think there's nothing lower than a janitor. You get the feeling that they're looking down on you because you're working for them. . . .
Interviewer: Well, why do you say you get the feeling that they are looking down on you? Why do you feel so sensitive?
Janitor: In different places you hear people talk janitor this and janitor that, and they say they'd never be a . . . janitor. So you think people here must say and think the same, but not to you. It makes you feel funny sometimes.

For the most part, those who occupy low status positions are insulted indirectly and subtly by the recognition that their occupation is held in low esteem. Only occasionally do these attitudes surface in the form of direct insults. This contrasts with the much more formalized ways in which low-status persons are insulted in caste and aristocratic societies. However, it is questionable whether the greater subtlety of such insults in modern egalitarian societies means that the subjective effects are qualitatively different. Gold's interviews tend to support the idea that the humiliations that low-status persons feel in modern society are just as painful as those experienced by the lower classes in traditional societies. Indeed, the subjective effects in a modern egalitarian context may be even more severe because of the widely held belief that a person can be anything he wants to be, and hence his low occupational prestige must result from lack of ambition or from individual shortcomings.

Thus, insults that derogate one's occupational prestige or social status are directed both at the individual and at the social category which he represents. But occupational status is primarily an achieved status; in American society, despite contrary ideologies, many statuses are essentially ascribed. This is particularly true of minority group memberships. Blacks, for example, are subjected to continual direct and indirect insults aimed at reconfirming the cultural definition of their "innate" inferiority and, perhaps most significantly, of seeking to continually remind them of, and hence internalize within them, a sense of the low social esteem in which they are held. There are many other essentially ascriptive groups that are also subjected to such insults—women, Jews, Indians, and so on, all of whom experience varied degrees of derogation, from the most blatant to the very subtle. Let us attempt to determine how these phenomena relate to the survival of ascriptive status orders in modern egalitarian societies.

Collective Insult: Keeping Minorities "In Their Place"

To this point we have been examining insults directed primarily against particular, unique individuals. Many insults, however, are clearly group-related in that they abuse a person not because of any unique traits which he or she supposedly possesses, but rather because of the characteristics which the person allegedly exhibits as a member of a specific minority group. "You are a stupid fool!" is an insult which refers to the supposed lack of judgment or ability of a particular individual. "You dumb nigger!" insinuates that the object is dumb because he is a black person, rather than because of his uniquely individual capacities.

Minority groups may be defined as subgroups within a society that are subject to prejudice, discrimination, segregation, and persecution. Thus, minorities are typically assigned to the lowest levels of the social ladder. Countless studies have examined the nature and causes of prejudice, discrimination, and the other manifestations of the minorities' plight. But few have recognized the role of collective insult as an important vehicle for the expression of prejudice, as well as a significant means of sustaining a system of social stratification that depends, in part, upon the maintenance of a cultural definition of minorities as inherently inferior.

Collective insult is a prime example of prejudice. Through subjection to collective insults, an individual member of a minority group is prejudged not as an individual person, but on the basis of negative traits supposedly characteristic of his or her group. In modern democratic societies, collective insults appear in a somewhat less blatant manner than in caste societies, as collective insults are less ritualized and formalized than the elaborate kinds of humiliation directed against the lowest social levels in rigidly stratified caste and aristocratic societies. In the American South, until perhaps fairly recently, blacks were subject to continual collective insults and humiliations—being called "boy" or "girl," having to wait in line while whites were waited on first, and so on—which continually reaffirmed their low social status and the caste-culture's definition of blacks as innately inferior. In the North, and perhaps in more progressive parts of the South, collective insult has by no means disappeared: what has changed is the degree of ritualization through which such group derogations are expressed.

Through interviews with a number of blacks living in the North, we were able to gain some understanding of the kinds of insults to which minority group members in a modern urbanized context are subjected. In a survey conducted by myself and two assistants, a random sampling of black students at Miami University were asked to give examples of collective insults they had experienced. In addition, the subjects were asked to indicate whether their reaction to the insult had been one of complete passivity, overt violence against the insulter, or somewhere between the two. The following are some of the experiences of collective insult afforded by the subjects of the study:

I pulled up to a traffic light in a friend's new car when an adult white male yelled out: "That nigger must have stolen that car."

I was walking to campus when I passed two white kids about ten years old whom I overheard say "damn niggers." I reacted passively and just walked on.

I was called a "dumb nigger" by a group of white youths as I passed them on the street, I was angry enough to hit one of them but I just pretended I didn't hear them.

I played cornet in high school and had first chair when I was a sophomore. In order to get first chair you had to challenge the person who held it and beat him. Well, I challenged the person and beat him.

Afterward, he said to me, "You know, Glenn, it wasn't your musical ability that beat me, it was those big lips you have. You know the characteristics of you people. How could I compete fairly with you?"

Last summer I was working in a factory. It was about 100 degrees out and I was unloading trucks. I stopped to rest a minute, when I heard one of the older white guys say: "Look at that lazy black son-of-a-bitch sitting on his ass."

One night there were three of us (two Whites and one Black) riding around. We saw another friend and he said hop in. We started to do so and he had a whole bunch of junk in the back seat so only one person could ride in the rear. The driver said "Jim, you can ride nigger since after all you are one" [Davis and Hamelberg, 1973].

A characteristic common to each of these examples of collective insult is their spontaneity. Unlike such insults that occur in a caste or traditional-class society, none of the above examples has any ritual character; nor are they as patterned or structured as the kinds of elaborate physical-avoidance insults typical of the relations between higher and lower castes in India and the traditional American South which we have already discussed. Nonetheless, the responses of the college students to the question "How did you react to the insult?" indicates that the subjective effect of the type of spontaneous, unstructured collective insults found in modern societies with an egalitarian ideology is at least as severe as the effects of more ritualized insults directed against members of the lower castes in a traditional context. Though none of the respondents in our survey reacted in a violent manner to the insults they experienced, several indicated that they were angered enough to strike out physically at the offenders, but stopped just short of doing so. Not all instances of collective insult, however, are greeted with a passive response. Depending upon the particular circumstances and upon the temperament of the individual who is collectively insulted, an offensive remark may well be greeted with vehement counterinsult or even violence. In one instance, for example, a first-generation American Jew named Perlmutter recalls an encounter with an older man which stopped short of violence only because of the advanced age of the offender. One day Perlmutter went out to buy a newspaper in his German-Jewish neighborhood. He encountered an old man who warned him not to go into a particular candy store: "It's a Yiddish store," Perlmutter was informed. "Jews own it. Stinking Jews! Don't go in there." Perlmutter at first reacted with shock, but in a few seconds he reacted with angered invective: "My own neighborhood . . . a loud Jewish hater. You sonofabitch! I'm Jewish, damn you, and if you weren't older than me I'd punch you in the nose!" The older man reasserted that Jews are filth, and also retorted that no Jew could lay a hand on him, whereupon Perlmutter angrily walked into the store and bought his paper [Perlmutter, 1972:35–39].

Such vehement counterinsult is essential if the minority group member is to maintain his self-respect. Even seemingly minor incidents of collective insult can have strong and deleterious psychological effects not only on the particular individual minority member who is thus offended, but upon others who are close to him. One of the most famous incidents of anti-Semitic collective insult involved Sigmund Freud's father, who was walking along the street one day when a Gentile stopped him and, making some insulting remarks about Jews, knocked the elder Freud's hat off into the gutter. When his father told the boy Sigmund what had happened, the latter asked, "Well, what did you do?" His father replied, "What could I do? I just went into the street and picked up my hat." This incident, and in particular his father's failure to respond to the insult in an active manner, deeply affected the young Freud. Previous to that point, he had regarded his father as a heroic figure, but the passivity that the elder Freud displayed in the face of collective insult caused Sigmund to become decidedly ambivalent toward his father [Puner, 1959:41]. The impact that the incident indirectly exerted on Freud's theories, with their strong emphasis on ambivalence toward the father, is but one notable instance of the long-lasting and strong effects that seemingly trivial instances of collective insult can have on minority group members.

In addition to reacting with passivity, counterinsult, and violence, some minority group members react in a formalized way to collective insult. Such a response is possible, however, in a societal context in which there are specific legal channels available. A black professor, for example, attempted to rent a house in the same university town to which he was moving. A real estate salesman accepted the professor's check as deposit, but later the head salesman and owner of the firm attempted to renege on the deal. When the black scholar replied, "Are you trying to tell me that they [his prospective neighbors] don't want me to move in?" the realtors admittedly expressed uneasiness as to the possible reactions of neighbors. The professor thereupon wrote a letter to the local newspaper which stated, in part, "It's tragic that a black man has to be three times as qualified as a white to live in a neighborhood like ———. The possibility of my renting a house there seemed to irritate [the realtor] because he himself had once lived along that street." In addition to writing letters of protest, the professor also reported the incident to the Ohio Civil Rights Commission and made sure that everyone in the small town, particularly his colleagues, knew about the insulting way in which he had been treated by the realty company. Such an active response is possible, however, only in those societies which provide the necessary formal channels. Such channels are, unfortunately, much more the exception than the rule, even in those societies, such as the United States, which have an ideological commitment to egalitarianism despite everyday normative standards that tend to undermine such ideals.

One example of the use of formal legal channels for the redress of collective insult involved the efforts of the B'nai B'rith, a Jewish organization, to combat the many insulting statements set forth in Henry Ford's newspaper *The Dearborn Independent.* Ford had used his privately owned newspaper as a medium for the expression of his anti-Semitic views. The Jewish community was offended by his many insulting comments about them and brought a class action suit against Ford on behalf of the Jewish population. This eventually led to a formal apology by Ford and the cessation of publication of the newspaper [Wittenberg, 1947:223]. Such use of legal channels as a response to collective insult against an entire minority group is, however, very rare. Much more prevalent has been the development of minority group consciousness among many people, particularly since the beginning of the Black Revolution in the late 1950s and early 1960s.

A significant correlate of the development of such awareness has been a tendency for minority groups to become increasingly sensitive to acts, remarks, and gestures, as well as media portrayals, that might be considered offensive. In other words, what the members of such groups had most often overlooked in the era previous to the development of minority group consciousness, they later came to define as offensive and insulting. For example, during the 1930s there were many motion pictures which portrayed black people as silly, immature, cowardly, and stupid, such as the Steppin Fetchit films. Such portrayals were, at the time, regarded simply as humorous. Contemporary blacks, however, have become aware that many of the ways in which they are portrayed in the media have been and are extremely disparaging and directly or indirectly insulting. In an article by the noted black psychiatrist Alvin F. Poussaint, it was pointed out that even in the supposedly positive portrayal of blacks in movies such as *Shaft* and others featuring supermasculine black heroes there are numerous—albeit more subtle—denigrations of black people. As Poussaint points out, "negative black stereotypes are far more subtle and neatly camouflaged than they were in the films of yesteryear, but the same insidious message is there: blacks are violent, criminal, sexy savages who imitate the white man's ways as best they can from their disadvantaged sanctuary in the ghetto" [Poussaint, 1974:26]. Poussaint's rejection of what he terms "blaxploitation" films is based largely on his view that they have substantial negative effects upon black adolescents, who, lacking positive male role models in the "real world" are encouraged to identify with the violent, and often criminal and antisocial heroes in the new films. Moreover, many blacks have taken offense at the portrayal of black people in a large number of films as dope dealers, prostitutes, and other fringe-element types. On occasion protests have taken the form of efforts by black organizations to prevent the distribution of films demeaning to blacks. In 1975, for example, the producer of an animated cartoon dealing with ghetto life was prevented from distributing his film through the efforts of CORE. The white producer of the film, in addition to his obvious chagrin at the financial losses that he sustained, was also very troubled by CORE's response to the film, since the producer had felt that he had presented a very pro-black message [*New York Times*, July 20, 1975]. In addition, groups other than blacks have been successful in efforts to prevent film makers from portraying them in an insulting or offensive manner. A prime example was the success of the Italian-American Civil Rights League in preventing the use of the term *Mafia* in the film *The Godfather* as well as in other films and television shows. This relatively recent sensitivity is, therefore, an important aspect and manifestation of the way in which insult behavior is related to the efforts of minority groups to actualize more fully American ideals of equality and social justice. This pattern is also characteristic of many deviant groups whose patterns of organized (as well as individual level) response to collective insult we will examine in the following chapter.

5

INSULT AND DEVIANCY

Every society has a set of values and norms to which its individuals are expected to conform. If substantial numbers of individuals act in ways contrary to general value guidelines or the specific normative prescriptions, the system is obviously threatened. Hence, every social system has certain methods whereby it attempts to ensure the conformity of its members to its behavioral expectations by making it painful for those who do not conform. Insult is one such control mechanism.

Use of Insult to Ensure Conformity

The basic patterns whereby nonconformists and deviants are subjected to ridicule and insult are essentially similar in primitive, traditional, and modern contexts. The major differences lie in the degree of formalization and institutionalization of the abuse. In primitive societies, as might be expected because of their relatively low degree of institutional differentiation, social control is carried out in a less formal manner than in traditional or modern societies. Usually, insult against deviants takes the form of ridicule, and deviants are used as negative references for children. Among the Yoruba tribespeople, for example, lazy persons are not only criticized and insulted, but are used as the butt of jokes by parents who wish to teach their children to be industrious [Bascom, 1951:492]. Among the Warao Indians, industrious members insult the weak ones with the word *Guanarao*, which means "Indian without canoe," or idler [Turrado Moreno, 1945:14]. Actual crime is dealt with in a somewhat more formalized fashion, but nonetheless without the institutional framework characteristic of traditional and modern legal systems. Moreover, the cultural meanings attached to criminal acts are often quite different from the ways in which such acts are defined in traditional and modern contexts. In Western Samoa, for example, a person who steals fruit from another is punished severely, not so much for the actual loss involved but because of the cultural meanings associated with the theft. To the natives of Samoa, any plant or tree that is deliberately damaged or stolen from is held to represent the actual body of its owner. Thus the theft of fruit from or mutilation of a tree or plant constitutes a grave insult to its owner, particularly if it is damaged in such a way as to render it useless for further propagation [Grattan, 1948:172].

Punishment for such acts often involves retribution of a kind which might appear at first to be relatively nonformalized, but its severity becomes apparent when one is made aware of the cultural meanings that are attached to it. Malinowski's study of punishment meted out to offenders among the Trobriand Islanders is a good example of the kind of retribution that might, from the traditional or modern reference point, appear mild, but is nevertheless quite devastating to those who understand and share in its cultural meaning. One such deceptively simple punishment found in the Trobriand society is banishment, accompanied by ridicule and insult. Typically, the deviant is assailed by the headman of the village in a loud voice: "You are a cause of trouble! You have done us harm. You have told lies. We do not want you to stay here. Go away! We drive you away!" Such words are spoken in strong emotion and are very rarely uttered. They have a very distinct cultural meaning which extends to them a binding force and an almost ritual power. A man who would try to accept passively the dreadful insult involved in them and remain in spite of them, would be dishonored forever. Hence, in spite of the apparent "simplicity" of such usage of insult against an offender, it serves as an effective punishment and social control device [Malinowski, 1929:120].

In traditional and modern societies, insult and humiliation of an offender is just as devastating, but is carried out in a more formalized manner. For example, before the advent of the penal system, offenders were humiliated and insulted by being placed in stocks or otherwise identified in some conspicuous manner, such as adulterous women having to wear a scarlet letter indicating their "sin" and exposing them to the ridicule and ostracism of the community. In modern societies, insult-punishment still takes place on an informal level. But in the case of serious offenses, the humiliation is more closely associated with the stigma of being in prison. In other words, the informal insult and humiliation that a modern offender suffers has been replaced not so much by more formalized social control procedures; rather, the context within which it takes place is more closely associated with the stigma of having been formally incarcerated. Thus, distinction between the kinds of insult to which offenders and deviants are subjected in primitive, traditional, and modern societies is of a contextual rather than qualitative nature.

The Effects of Insult upon Deviants and Offenders

Insulting a deviant or an offender is usually not an effective method of changing his behavior patterns. One reason for this lies in the fact that a great deal of deviant behavior takes place within a group context. Deviant and criminal behavior, according to most sociological studies, is for the most part carried out not by lone individuals, but by groups. Moreover, such collectivities very often constitute a subculture which has values and norms contradictory to those of the dominant society. Accordingly, insult and ridicule against those who engage in deviant behavior leads to a greater degree of cohesion and solidarity among the members of a deviant group because it forces them to band together in the face of hostility. In other words, attack from without leads to a strengthening of group cohesion as well as a reaffirmation of the deviant standards to which a deviant subculture adheres because of the necessity for common defense. Hence, insult and ridicule of a deviant group by a dominant culture often has the ironic effect of strengthening the very behavior patterns which the dominant society condemns. The insult and hostility that is directed toward convicts, for example, often serves not to dissuade offenders from further deviant behavior, but rather to solidify their hostility toward the dominant society. As a result, their proclivities toward engaging in anti-social behavior are reinforced rather than extinguished. This suggests that the latent purpose of the dominant society's punishment, through insult and ridicule of deviants, is not to dissuade offenders from their deviant ways, but instead to reinforce the values and norms of the dominant culture. In other words, insult against deviants functions not mainly to change the deviants' behavior so much as to reassert and reaffirm the values and norms of the dominant society.

In a very real sense "deviance" does not exist unless the members of a sociocultural system single out and label certain kinds of behavior as wrong or criminal. Insult is one means of showing disapproval of behavior patterns that have been so labelled. Moreover, the very act of insulting some person or group who exhibits deviant behavior serves to reinforce and sustain the dominant society's definitions of what is valuable and normatively proper. Thus, insult and ridicule directed at deviants tends not only to strengthen their commitment to nonconforming ways by creating greater subcultural cohesion, but also to reaffirm the dominant culture's commitment to its standards.

What about the individual member of the dominant culture who insults deviants? What kinds of social-psychological functions does such abuse serve for him? Often, the individual who insults deviants does so in order to gain status within his own group by making a display of his own conformity to its values and norms. Southern politicians, for example, have long used insult and abuse against blacks as a means of gaining status and power from their racist white constituents; by insulting blacks, they affirm their own conformity to the values of white supremacy and the norms of racial segregation. Similar patterns can be found among boys or men who make a display of abusing homosexuals; their abuse—both verbal and physical—of "fags" is often an attempt to gain status with their "normal" male peers by appearing tough and masculine. According to Dennis Altman, for example, "It is generally true that what has been termed 'the authoritarian personality' does display a consistent hatred of all out-groups, and that the homosexual, under some circumstances, becomes a convenient scapegoat who can be accused of responsibility for all sorts of moral degeneracy" [Altman, 1971:69]. Another good example of the use of insult and ridicule of deviants to raise one's own status was the tirades of Joseph McCarthy against supposed Communists and "fellow travelers" during the fifties. McCarthy's actions were undoubtedly motivated in part by a desire to impress his constituents with his strong adherence to patriotic ideals. It was of course during this same post-World War II "red scare" era that Richard Nixon used techniques similar to those of Joseph McCarthy to attain political power and wide popular support that continued—via enemies lists and various other types of denigratory politiking—through to the last days of his presidency. The same socio-psychological dynamics were, of course, apparent in Hitler's use of insult against Jews to gain power and status among Germans. Another contemporary example: while a student at Berkeley, I witnessed an attempt to gain political status through the use of insult and abuse against deviants. One spring day, a Republican candidate for the governorship of California named William Penn Patrick visited the Berkeley campus with a phalanx of reporters and cameramen. Walking over to the card tables where various political groups were distributing literature, he roundly denounced them as being "beatniks" and "Communists." Then, the cameras still rolling, he went to a speaker's platform near the center of the campus and told of how "disgusted and appalled" he was at "all the lousy looking bums" that he had seen on the campus. About a week later, political campaign advertisements began to appear on television, with William Penn Patrick portrayed around the campus, denouncing and insulting students and reaffirming his commitment to the "good, old-fashioned American way" as evidenced in his fervent reiteration of such slogans as "my country, right or wrong." Patrick lost out to Ronald Reagan in his bid for the governorship; nonetheless, his campaign provided a clear illustration of the use of insult against deviants as a tool for gaining status vis-à-vis the insulter's own peers. Clearly Patrick and his ilk had no real desire to change or transform the deviant behavior of the Berkeley students; to immediately have them become conservative and well-scrubbed would have cost Patrick a potent political weapon.

Insult and the Projection of Undesirable Attributes

Besides providing possible status gains, insults against deviants by those who conform to the dominant culture may serve the function of denying the conformer's own unacceptable impulses and feelings by projecting them onto deviants. As Allport has pointed out, projection is a significant element in the expression of prejudice [Allport, 1958:360-84]. Typically, members of the dominant society are required to repress certain kinds of impulses and feelings, such as those pertaining to sexual interests or the desire to "goof off" rather than to be industrious. Many times individuals who are unsuccessful in their attempts to completely repress such desires tend to deny them, and instead attribute the same shortcomings to members of minority groups and deviants. Thus, in the South, the unacceptable sexual impulses and "lazy" tendencies that are unsuccessfully repressed by Protestant morality are projected onto the black population. Likewise, sexual desires and unacceptable needs for relief from the pressure of the "rat race" are projected onto the "hippies" and other deviants. In this way, the anger and loss of self-esteem that would otherwise be directed inward finds an outlet in the ridiculing and insulting of deviants who supposedly embody those traits which the prejudiced person finds undesirable in himself. Thus, as in the case of the prejudiced, dominant-culture conforming person who uses insult against deviants to raise his own status, the projecting person is not actually employing insult as a social control device, because he is not genuinely interested in transforming the behavior of the deviant; quite the contrary, he seeks its continuation and indeed "sees" it when it isn't there so that he will have some release for the hostility against the undesirable feelings and traits that he finds in himself but attributes to deviants.

Thus, in general, insult against deviants is only partially related to social control. As we have seen, insult and ridicule of deviants often does not serve to change their behavior, but rather tends to reinforce nonconforming patterns. And much of the insult directed at deviants is motivated not by a desire to change the deviants' behavior, but rather to perpetuate it so that: (1) dominant values and norms can be reaffirmed, (2) the insulter might gain status within his own reference group, and (3) the dominant group might have social objects upon which to project their unacceptable feelings and desires.

The Development of Gay Awareness

The relatively recent refusal to accept insults is manifest in two general patterns of response to insult among deviants. Since homosexuals are a prime example of a deviant group which has developed a substantial degree of unwillingness to accept insults passively, let us focus on new patterns in the development of minority group consciousness among homosexuals that has occurred largely since the 1960s. Since the development of a "gay awareness," homosexuals as individuals have increasingly come to regard their sexuality and life styles not as pathologically abnormal, but as valid and worthy of respect. Though there is substantial scholarly dispute over the sources of the self-hate that homosexuals experience, most gay activists believe that it is largely a product of the internalization of prevailingly negative social attitudes. Thus, it has become especially important for the homosexual to respond in kind (i.e., with counterinsult, if not active protest) to any insult directed against his or her homosexual identity. Such response may consist of humorous insult-banter between gays and straights, violent outbursts against the pervasive use of collective insults, and systematic and organized efforts to combat insulting and disparaging definitions of homosexuality.

Inspired largely by the efforts of blacks to obtain social justice, a wide variety of minority groups has increasingly fought back against the collective insults directed toward them by prevailing dominant-culture opinions. We have already explored the reasons for which members of the conforming society insult and in various other ways persecute and therefore "control" minority groups. Several organizations have been developed to combat the individual minority group member's tendencies to internalize, and hence accept as valid, insulting acts, remarks, and gestures. Organized groups such as the Gay Activists Alliance and the Gay Liberation Front have tried to negate prevailing opinions of homosexuals by attempting to eliminate job discrimination and by adopting various other methods of "striking back" at persecution. One example of the accomplishments of such organized and systematic protest was gay activists' successful attempt to obtain a change in the American Psychiatric Association's official view of homosexuality as a type of illness or "disorder." These groups and others have also engaged in sensationalistic demonstrations. For example, a member briefly disrupted a CBS evening news broadcast one evening to protest the insulting portrayals of homosexuals on some of the network's television programming. Violent response to insult has also been apparent among some gays. In one incident, cited by many gay activists as the real beginning of their movement, homosexuals resisted—actually fought—arresting police officers during a 1970 raid on a gay bar on Christopher Street in New York City. At about the same time, homosexuals in a number of cities began to form groups to fight back against gangs of straight youths who took pleasure in beating up homosexuals.

On the individual incident level, Richard Troiden provides the following examples of counterinsult against straights. In a restaurant a male homosexual was once insulted by a woman who mocked his effeminate mannerisms and remarked, "Look at that fag!" The gay replied, "That's right, dearie, I may not be straight, but I'm hell of a more of a lady than you are!" In another incident, a homosexual was asked by a patronizing acquaintance when he had first become aware that he was not "normal." The insulted gay replied, "Tell me, when did you first become aware of your heterosexuality?" Such incidents are significant in that they illustrate homosexuals' growing awareness of the offensive nature underlying many of the stereotypical attitudes that have previously not been regarded as offensive, and homosexuals have begun to liberate themselves by striking back against insulters [Troiden, personal communication].

According to Dennis Altman, perhaps the most common form of oppression to which the homosexual is exposed is the patronizing tolerance of would-be liberals. "The difference between tolerance and acceptance," argues Altman, "is considerable, for tolerance is a gift extended by the superior to the inferior. . . . Such an attitude is far different from acceptance, which implies not that one pities others . . . but rather that one accepts the equal validity of their style of life" [Altman, 1971:50-51].

We have seen how insult behavior can be used, although sometimes unsuccessfully, to "control" the behavior of minority groups which have been regarded by the dominant sociocultural group to be deviant. Are there ways, however, in which insult actually does serve as a major means of social control in primitive, traditional, and modern societies? Let us examine the relationship between insult, legal systems, and religion.

6

LEGAL SYSTEMS, RELIGION, AND INSULT BEHAVIOR

Legal institutions are related to insult behavior in two basic ways. First, in most societies the law provides possibilities for gaining legal redress for insult-related grievances. If a person has been insulted so that his reputation or material interests have been seriously damaged, the legal system of most societies provides mechanisms for him to react in a formal, nonviolent manner. Second, a legal system may constrain an insulted person from responding in a violent manner, by failing to support such forms of retaliation.

There are substantial differences between sociocultural systems either in the degree to which their legal frameworks provide a means of redress against an insulter, or in the degree to which their laws condone violent response. These functional differences are apparent both between the three general types of societies we have been examining (tribal-village, caste-estate, and modern industrialized) and within these three categories. Let us examine the different ways in which the legal systems of various societies are related to insult behavior.

Insult and Law in the Tribal-Village Context

Many tribal and village societies provide specific legal penalties against insult. In general, based on the evidence we have obtained from ethnographic accounts, interpersonal and interfamilial insults are a more serious offense than in modern societies because of the central importance of individual and family honor in the relatively small-scale tribal and village context. Social status is much more particularistic in such societal milieu, because it is based upon an individual's or a family's reputation, than in modern societies where universalistic, essentially impersonal criteria constitute the major bases of status. To an Ashanti tribesman of Africa, for example, having a good name is well-nigh essential to existence. Hence, the Ashanti is extremely sensitive to personal insults that could cause him to have a bad name in the narrow community in which he lives. Public ridicule and insult are such serious matters to the Ashanti that any individual who is subjected to them is very likely to commit suicide, since life in his small community has become unbearable to him. In a larger-scale society, it would of course be possible for an insulted individual simply to ignore and withdraw from his tormentor. The impossibility of such passive response in the Ashanti society is one significant reason why the tribe has developed a relatively complex set of legal proceedings that are invariably and immediately followed by offended parties in instances of personal abuse, slander, and insult [Rattray, 1929:309].

Tribal-village societies differ in the degree of complexity of their insult-related litigation processes. A relatively informal process of legal response to insult is found among the Trobriand Islanders. According to Malinowski, the rare quarrels that occur among the Islanders usually take the form of a public expostulation in which the parties involved, supported by friends and relatives, publicly harangue one another and hurl mutual recriminations. Such litigation allows them to give vent to their feelings in a nonviolent manner which does not disrupt the ongoing social processes and which effectively heads off the possibility of a vicious circle of violence, revenge, and feuding [Malinowski, 1926:60].

In some societies, the legal system imposes fines upon the insulter. Among the Formosan aborigines, a person who has made a slanderous remark is at first requested to retract it and to ask for pardon. A refusal to do so means that the offender will be forced to pay a fine to the insulted party [Plaut, 1903:12]. In some Indonesian village cultures, the legal penalties against insult are relatively complex: fines are established in relation to the degree of seriousness of the insult. These fines involve three plates for an ordinary insult, three plates and a pig for a serious insult, and ten plates for insulting a chief. A number of Vietnamese village societies also provide specific kinds of sanctions for various kinds of insults. In the Vietnamese village of Co-Ninh in the Tonkin province, for example, every person who is at odds with another must address the grievance to the village chief. If a person insults someone instead of going to the chief, he must pay a fine. In addition, noninvolvement of neighbors is not tolerated as it is in more "civilized" societies: neighbors who fail to intervene in a dispute involving mutual insults must also pay a fine to the village chief [Nguyen Van Khoan, 1942:2-3].

The laws of many tribal and village societies function to uphold and maintain the existing status order by imposing more severe penalties for insults against persons of status higher than the insulter. In many societies the legal system, by imposing unequal penalties for insults that implicitly threaten the social order, is one medium whereby the social control of insult behavior is directly related to the maintenance of stratification patterns. Thus, it appears that one purpose of legal prohibition and penalties against insult is to preserve the social system against implicit attacks upon the established order that are manifest in insults directed against those who occupy positions of high social standing, either within the society as a whole or within smaller contexts such as the family. For example, lower status Vietnamese individuals who insult their social superiors are more heavily penalized than those who insult their social equals or inferiors. Young Vietnamese who have insulted superiors or aged persons, or women who have insulted their husbands, are punished with a fine double the usual amount. Even more serious in Ashanti tribal society is any abuse or slander of a head chief or any of his dead ancestors. Due to the chief's peculiarly sacred position, such insults are considered a tribal taboo and are punished severely in the rare instances of their occurrence [Rattray, 1929:309].

Some tribal and village societies do not have formalized legal systems that provide sanctions against insults. In many such societies, religion and magic provide a kind of functional equivalent to legal means of redress in insult-related grievances. Let us examine how religion functions as a supernatural control over insult behavior in several different tribal and village societies.

Religion and Magic as Functional Equivalents of Law in Tribal-Village Societies

In many tribal and village cultures, religion and the supernatural are functionally related to the control of insult behavior. First, religion and witchcraft provide an indirect means of responding to insults. By using magic and performing ritual curses against those who have insulted him or her, an insulted person is able to avoid direct, violent response against an offender. Such use of the supernatural as a response to insult also has the positive social side-effect of avoiding the threats to the solidarity of the tribe or village posed by overt violence. Secondly, the supernaturalization of response to insult constitutes a powerful social control mechanism that is functionally equivalent to the attempt of secular legal systems to deter insult: the possibility of a supernatural response to insult means that an offender has to face and contend with not only the person he has insulted, but also the supernatural forces which the offended party is able to invoke against the tormentor. Let us look at some examples of the use of religion as an equivalent of legal response to insult in the absence of secular means of redress.

A good example of a supernatural symbolic system providing an alternative to legal response is found in the African tribal society of Ganda, where it is taken for granted that a person with a legitimate grievance for which he or she can get no other satisfaction will resort to sorcery. Just as an offended person in a modern society might go to a lawyer, the Ganda tribesman visits a reputable magician, who prescribes, for a fee, the correct type of spells and curses to inflict upon the insulter [Mair, 1934:252]. A similar pattern exists among the Maori, whose fear of supernatural retribution serves as an effective deterrent of insult. In instances where Maori are insulted, the magical rites designed to cast a spell against the insulter are so impressive that they often cause the offender to abandon his home and leave the district. Such Maori rituals are quite elaborate: for example, a wizard hollows out a small pit in the earth and puts his head in it, keeping it there as he repeats the words of the spell [Best, 1924:334].

In many societies whose role structures do not include magicians or wizards, witchcraft serves as an effective substitute for both legal and magical response to insult, as well as constituting an effective deterrent. Among the Azande tribespeople of Africa, for example, belief in witchcraft is a valuable corrective to uncharitable impulses, since an insult may cause serious repercussions. In Azande society, the very ambiguity of the role and identity of witches is a significant part of witchcraft's effectiveness as an insult-deterrent. Since the Azande do not know who are and who are not witches, they assume that all their neighbors may be witches and are thus careful not to offend any of them without good cause [Evans-Pritchard, 1929:112]. A similar utilization of witchcraft as a deterrent to insult is found among the Sanpoil Indian tribe of the American Northwest, where there is no direct taboo against quarreling, but care has to be taken about insulting another or incurring his ill will for fear that he or she might have supernatural powers and thus be able to inflict misfortunes as retaliations [Ray, 1933:124].

The fear of supernatural powers serves in many cultures to protect older members of the tribe or village. Old persons are often viewed as the most likely holders of supernatural power; hence, younger members' fear of their supernatural abilities allows old people a certain defense against insult and ridicule which they would not otherwise be able to possess because of their relative inability to respond to insult in an overt, violent manner. In this sense, advanced age of older members of many tribes allows them to be spared the full measure of abuse that might be directed toward them in the absence of their culturally defined supernatural powers. A good example of the way supernaturalism can serve as a protection for old people is afforded by Hallowell's account of a customary warning given by Saulteaux Indian fathers to their children: "Don't laugh at old people. Don't say to any old person that he is ugly. If that person has magical power, he can make you ugly also." There is no abstract ethical ideal involved for the child in avoiding insults against old people—avoidance of offense is simply a matter of defense [Hallowell, 1955:284].

Thus, in cultures that lack secular, legal systems to ensure older people the necessities of life, the supposed supernatural capacities of old people function as a means of making sure that the younger members of the tribe or village do not forget their responsibilities to their elders. In some tribes, no one dares to insult an old person by not offering him any beer or not sharing meat with him. If an old man possessing supernatural powers receives no meat, he will prevent the killing of any more animals.

Displacement of Response to the Supernatural Realm

In addition to providing a deterrent against insult, in many tribal and village societies supernaturalism also provides a clear equivalent of legal response to insult. Just as the legal system of industrialized societies serves in part to provide a mechanism whereby violent and hence socially disruptive responses to insult might be kept at a minimum, thus supernaturalism provides for many tribal and village societies a means of minimizing the occurrence of insult-related violence by displacing aggression to the supernatural realm. This displacement effect works two ways. First, the supernatural realm serves as a locus for the redirection of aggressive retaliation away from the offender; potentially disruptive violence is thereby avoided. Second, persons whom the society defines as witches can serve as scapegoats for those who seek redress for being insulted or ridiculed. In both instances, the supernaturalization of response to insult constitutes a functional equivalent for legal retribution in that it allows tribal and village societies to "keep the peace" in the absence of formal legal institutions comparable to those of modern societies.

In the Maori tribal culture of New Zealand, for example, quarrels and feuds are prevented from developing into overt violence by redirecting response to insult into the spiritual realm. If two men quarrel, their guardian spirits are said to have quarreled; if a man dies, the guardian ghost of someone he has offended is held responsible. In this way, the offense is depersonalized; it is not an insulted possessor of black magic who causes an offender to be punished, it is rather the force of the magic. In a similar fashion, an offended individual attributes any ill effects that might result from an insult to the sinfulness of the offender, which can of course be influenced only by magical means. By displacing and depersonalizing the causes of offense, the Maori culture provides a mechanism for preventing overt, violent retaliation against an insulter [Best, 1924:334]. A similar pattern of substituting the supernatural for violent retaliation against insult and abuse is found in the Arande society, one of the Australian aboriginal tribes, where it is customary to avoid overt aggression by using magical influences to bring about the downfall of an offender. The Aranda method involves the "wonderfully potent" practice of "pointing" death at a man, who may or may not be present or visible. This form of magical curse is referred to as "pointing the bone," or simply "boning" [Basedow, 1925:174].

In other cultures, the supernatural mode of response does not necessarily involve the suggestive power of magic or a curse of death, but rather the wish that the gods punish the offender. In one Vietnamese village society, for example, a person who feels he has been offended by another asks the offender (if he has denied the accusation) to take an oath before the altar of a spirit. Both parties ask that the true offender be punished by the spirit. Once the ritual takes place before the altar, the quarrel is ended and retribution for any offense is left to the gods. In this manner, overt violence is avoided in much the same way that secularized legal systems of modern industrialized societies provide formalized means of short-circuiting violent response to insults both by providing a means of ascertaining whether an offense has been committed, and determining the proper punishment [Rouilly, 1929:20].

Witches as Scapegoats for Insult-Related Hostility

In his analysis of Navaho tribal society, Kluckhohn emphasizes the role of witchcraft as a means of redirecting aggressive response to insult and abuse [Kluckhohn, 1944]. The sociocultural system of the Navahos, according to Kluckhohn, places great normative restraint upon the overt expression of hostility through violence. The role of the witch in Navaho society involves two closely related functions, both of which constitute the functional equivalents of legal systems found in industrialized societies. First of all, the witch is the only legitimate object of insult and abuse in a society which does not otherwise legitimate interpersonal hostility. The witch is the person whom, the ideal patterns of the culture say, it is not only proper but necessary to hate. Instead of saying all the bitter and insulting things he has felt against, for example, his father-in-law, the Navaho avoids the social disapproval and economic consequences of such recrimination by redirecting his hostility against a totally unrelated witch in the community. Thus, the scapegoat role of the witch serves both to maintain family and kin group solidarity within the tribe and to prevent disruptive violence and feuding between the various kin groups within the community. A second, closely related function of the role of witches in Navaho society is its provision of a legitimate object for responding to abuse and insult. A Navaho who has been offended is, by and large, constrained by the Navaho norms which proscribe overt retaliation from responding in a direct manner to an insult. The only means of response open to him is to define the insult as having been caused by the evil influence of a witch upon the offender. Thus, the culture provides a means whereby the hostility engendered by abuse or insult can be directed away from the actual offender onto the culturally defined source of the insult—the witch-scapegoat.

Why do the Navahos, as well as many other tribal-village societies, place such a strong emphasis on inhibiting and controlling the overt expression of hostility and insult-related aggression by providing supernatural means both for responding to insults and for abusing others? Kluckhohn maintains that the Navaho cultural patterns of prohibition of violence and hostility can be explained in terms of the actual helplessness of many people in a scattered and inadequately policed society. Such circumstances, together with the lack of a legal system capable of providing protection against abuse or retaliation against perceived insult, make the playing down of overt aggression on the part of most tribal and village peoples a highly adaptive response. Is the same adaptive function true of the laws pertaining to insult and response to insult in more complex societies? Let us look at how the legal frameworks of the American South differ from those of tribal and village societies and from the modern industrialized societies' methods of insult control.

Insult and the Law in the American South

As we have already mentioned in an examination of the institution of duelling, the traditional American South exhibited many characteristics of the typical caste-estate systems. The South has always placed a great value upon the maintenance of individual honor. This subcultural pattern is particularly true in Texas, where certain characteristics of the Southern caste system are combined with the frontier subculture. Although Texas is now becoming increasingly urbanized and homogenized with the dominant American culture, there have been and still are some significant differences between the statutes of Texas and of other non-Southern states in relation to the norms regarding violent response to insult. An interesting example is the subcultural differentiation evinced by the Texas insult-related statutes. In American common law as a whole, provocative and insulting words are not recognized as adequate provocation to reduce a charge of homicide to one of manslaughter, no matter how "abusive, aggravating, contemptuous, false, grievous, indecent, insulting, opprobrious, provoking or scurrilous" the words might be, according to the Corpus Juris Secundum. The few exceptions to this rule of common law are found in cases that occurred in the South. One prominent exception was a Texas statute repealed in the 1930s which stated that insulting words or insulting conduct by the person killed, directed toward a female relative of the perpetrator of a murder, was a sufficient cause to have a charge of homicide reduced to one of manslaughter. In this instance we see very clearly the influence of the Southern subculture upon laws governing violent response to insult. Since the South has always valued the honor of its womanhood, the law until relatively recently has tended at least in Texas to support those who avenge any attempts to cast aspersions upon that honor. We are reminded of the duel between the two judges in Arkansas which resulted because one of them had "slighted the honor of a lady."

In general, the subcultural norms of the South are much more lenient than the legal norms of the non-Southern states toward violent response to insult. Such a response is much more likely to occur in, say, Texas or Arkansas than in New York. Among New York City inhabitants, it is well known that the law provides little or no support for someone who reacts violently to insult; the law requires one to walk away from another who is attempting to provoke a fight.

This subcultural contrast can be highlighted by comparing the judge's opinion in an Arkansas case with a similar case in California. According to the Southern judge, "Insulting words . . . may be considered in determining the degree of murder, or in assessing the punishment of murder, if the law provides more than one possible penalty." In a 1956 California decision, on the other hand, it was ruled that "provocative words . . . cannot justify or excuse an assault likely to produce great bodily injury" [People v. Mears, 1956].

There are substantial subcultural differences in the extent to which insults can be made the basis of legal action. In most of the United States, a person cannot take action against another merely for having been insulted. The law requires that some definite damage have been done to an individual's business or professional reputation before he can be afforded legal redress for insult-related grievances. An exception to this can be found in Mississippi; there, according to a particular legal statute, words which from their usual construction and common acceptance are construed as insults and tend to breach the peace are actionable. In contrast to other states, which make no legal provision for the damages to an insulted person's feelings, the Mississippi statute maintains that the basis for insult-related legal action is the "insult to the feelings of the offended person, rather than the intention of the person using the [insulting] words." Let us look for a moment at a particular case in which the Mississippi statutes pertaining to insult and response to insult were applied. The case involved a man named Nash who came into a store run by a Mr. Huckabee to complain about the weight of a chicken which Huckabee had sold earlier to Nash's servant. According to witnesses, Nash felt he had been cheated and began arguing heatedly with Huckabee. In the course of the argument Nash drew a pistol and pointed it at Huckabee, saying to him, "You God damned son of a bitch." Huckabee reached for a knife that was lying on a counter and rushed at Nash with it. Nash, threatening with his pistol, ordered Huckabee to drop the knife. He complied, whereupon Nash put his pistol back in his pocket and walked out of the store. Interestingly enough, the court case that arose out of this incident had nothing to do with the threats and counterthreats of violence, but with whether or not Nash, who first insulted Huckabee, could obtain damages against Huckabee for having been the object of a counterinsult. The problem revolved around the fact that after having been insulted by Nash, Huckabee returned the insult by using the same language against Nash during the argument. The judge ruled that Nash could not collect because he had been the instigator of the verbal combat. As the ruling stated, one person cannot insult another and then expect to take legal action if the latter replies in kind. The significant point, however, is that Nash would even think that he could obtain damages [Huckabee v. Nash, 1938]. In other parts of the United States, the case would never even have made it to court because of the absence of any statutes that could make it possible to gain legal redress for having been insulted. It is also significant that the Mississippi court implicitly condoned the overt threats of violence of the two parties: that Nash and the legal authorities evidently considered the spoken insults more legally actionable than overt threats and narrowly averted mayhem tells us that the Southern subcultural norms evidently considered a spoken offense against one's honor more significant than a threat against a person's life.

Not surprisingly, the statutory definitions of libel vary substantially according to regions. The laws in various states of the American South, for example, clearly evidence vestiges of an aristocratic attitude. In North Carolina it is considered libellous "to destroy the reputation of innocent and unprotected women, whose very existence in society depends upon the unsullied purity of their character. . . ." But in states such as North and South Dakota (as well as in most other northern and western states), libel laws do not recognize the gender of the victim of a libelous action [Wittenberg, 1947:8–9]. A news item from the *Cincinnati Post* of July 15, 1975, shows how some of the Southern laws regarding insult behavior have been and continue to be changed:

James Dillard has won a new trial on murder charges because of an old Texas "paramour law" that allowed a husband to kill his wife's lover if he caught them committing adultery. The Texas Court of Criminal Appeals, in a 3–2 decision, reversed a five-year sentence against Shaw for the August 20, 1971 slaying of Eugene Hintz. The appeals court ruled that a Houston judge failed to tell the jury that convicted Shaw of the existence of the "paramour law" that since has been repealed under a new Texas penal code.

The subcultural differences that we have illustrated do represent the survival of certain features of the Southern subculture which derive fundamentally from the caste-estate type social order which has until relatively recently characterized the traditional Southern sociocultural order. And we have seen how the various possibilities of response to insult, as well as the degree of toleration of violent response, are different in most other regions of the United States. Americans are occasionally surprised to learn how other modern industrialized milieux have made legal provisions for dealing with insult phenomena. One example is provided by Peter Berger, who related an incident that took place as he was traveling with a friend along the German autobahn. At one point in the trip, Berger's companion, who was driving, was slow in getting out of the way of a car which wanted to pass in the fast lane. As the car passed, the evidently irritated driver of the other car turned around, and looking at Berger's friend, pointed to his own head to imply that Berger's friend was stupid. Berger was surprised when his companion recorded the other driver's license number and later reported the incident to the German equivalent of the state police. Sometime later, Berger inquired about the matter and found that the driver of the other car had received a citation for "insult on the autobahn" [Peter Berger, personal communication].

Libel and Insult in Modern Societies

A major difference between modern industrialized societies and traditional caste-estate societies is that the former emphasize contract relations and economic relationships, whereas in the latter a man's reputation and honor are generally more important as a basis of individual social status. The differential legal norms between the American South and the other regions reflect this basic difference between the two types of sociocultural systems. As we have seen, some Southern statutes allow an individual to take legal action against one who has insulted him personally. In other regions, however, legal action is possible against an insulter only if the insults were sufficient to damage the plaintiff's business or professional reputation. Insults that are personal and do not involve direct damage to one's economic interests are not legally actionable. Insult-related legal action in modern societies often centers around the attempt of the plaintiff to prove that a given insult has actually damaged his or her reputation enough to undermine economic interests. In such instances, insults become legally defined as libel.

An example of the ambiguity of application of libel laws and the difficulty of obtaining legal redress for insult and ridicule is afforded by the 1934 case of a well-known New York businessman and sportsman who accepted five hundred dollars to appear in a cigarette advertisement in which he was photographed sitting on a race horse, smoking the cigarette. When the ad appeared in a national magazine, the photograph showed a leather strap, part of the saddle, in such a way that the strap appeared to be part of the man's anatomy. The ad was worded in such a way ("Camels really perk me up!") that, together with the unfortunate placement of the leather strap, an obscene interpretation could hardly be avoided. Soon after the ad appeared, the businessman became the subject of joking and ridicule from his acquaintances, and the advertisement thus caused him a substantial amount of embarrassment. As a result, he sued the cigarette company and its advertising agency, as well as the magazines in which the ad appeared, on the grounds that he had been exposed to ridicule severe enough to cause him serious loss of his business reputation among his peers and hence to endure indirect material economic losses. The court agreed, and the plaintiff was awarded a small amount as restitution. In many essentially similar cases, however, people who have been insulted and ridiculed have not been able to prove that their economic interests have been damaged, and thus have not been able to obtain any type of formal redress of grievance.

Perhaps more interesting are the many cases of libel in which the object of the insult was able to collect damages for being accused of sexual and other general kinds of deviancy, not directly related to his or her business or profession. The tendency of any given legal system to find terms libellous is directly related to and reflected by the prevalent values and norms of the sociocultural context. Examples of this include the large number of instances in which Southern courts have considered libellous any imputation that a white person had Negro ancestry. In 1919, for example, it was considered libellous in Oklahoma when the term "colored" was mistakenly placed after the name of a patient in an institution. In 1900, 1905, and 1914, courts in Louisiana, South Carolina, and Virginia also found the terms "colored" and "Negro" to be libellous when applied to white men. Other kinds of accusations of deviance that proved libellous included women who were accused of having illegitimate children [Missouri, 1844; Virginia, 1940]; a man who was said to be a "seducer" [Illinois, 1902]; and a man about whom it was said "He was a man. At least his wife says he was. Doctors are doubtful" [Wisconsin, 1892; Wittenberg, 1947:286, 306-7].

7

PRIMARY RELATIONSHIPS, INSULT, AND HUMOR

An insult is commonly regarded as an expression of negative or hostile sentiment. But not all insults are intended to be antagonistic; indeed, insults can often serve as an indirect means of expressing affection or as a type of humor.

Insult and the Thin Line between Affection and Offense

If people are close enough to one another that they are able to kid each other in an insulting way, an exchange of insults may serve to both define and sustain their primary bonds. The use of insult as an indirect mode of expressing friendship and affection is particularly common among males, for whom the direct expression of friendship is considered awkward. In contemporary American culture, for example, male sex norms proscribe the direct expression of affection or primary sentiment among men. Consequently, buddies often use nonserious insults as a means of expressing friendship, while at the same time maintaining the "tough," nonfeminine, unsentimental posture expected of American males in their relationships with one another. Such use of insult as a means of reaffirming primary bonds is found in a wide variety of male groups in our society. In his book on the everyday life of the fireman, Dennis Smith offers a typical example of affectionate insult among the members of a cohesive male group:

"Yessir, men, Mrs. O'Mann is cooking Irish footballs tonight, and she requests that you clean off the tables."

Billy-o hears the remark, and approaches waving a long-pronged fork in his hand. "Listen, Charlie," he says, "I don't mind you calling me Mrs. O'Mann, just as long as you don't try to touch my body."

"He doesn't need you, Billy-o," Jerry Herbert says, "because he can get his own Mrs. McCarthy for a deuce anytime he wants."

Everyone laughs. Charlie makes a motion as if he was pulling a spear from his chest. "Got me," he says. "But, a deuce is a lot of money. It doesn't cost that much, does it?"

"Well, it depends on whether you want coupons or not," Billy-o says.

Charlie, Billy-o, and Jerry have worked together for the past seven years—in fires and above fires, where it is roughest. Each has saved the other's life at one time or another, and they can say anything about each other, or each other's family, with impunity [Smith, 1972:17-18].

This insight into the way in which nonserious insults serve as a means of sustaining a sense of comradeship among firemen suggests that the degree of primary relationship between individuals or members of a group is an important variable in determining whether or not an act or remark will be defined as seriously insulting, or as "just kidding." In other words, the existence of a primary relationship between individuals or members of a group appears to create a more "permissive" interactional context in which joking and kidding can take place with less probability that the intended humor will be interpreted as an insult. Thus, humor and insult may serve to define the boundaries of friendship and, in an indirect manner, reinforce primary bonds. Specifically, as we have seen in the case of the firemen, individuals who are close friends may often kid one another in a manner that would constitute serious insult if used against those with whom they are not well acquainted or with whom they are not as close. The fact that individuals who do have a strong primary relationship are able to voice ostensibly serious insults to one another in the spirit of kidding without being taken seriously serves as one means not only to define the strength of, but to actually reinforce their primary ties.

In preparatory school, for example, I often witnessed two or more boys who were close buddies insult one another. The content and style of their bantering was, on the surface, very similar to the serious "slashing" that took place between boys who did not like one another and were trying to "cut each other down." These insults among friends, however, had entirely the opposite function from the more serious variety. Thus, Whitaker and Lack, two prep-school buddies, would often stand out in the corridor, engaging in a verbal duel such as the following:

"Whitaker, you are really a dumb shit!"

"You're such a dingleberry, Lack, that you couldn't even screw your mother right."

"What a spaz!"

These "insults," to be sure, merely served to underscore and reaffirm Whitaker and Lack's friendship; among boys who were not friends, they would no doubt have been taken seriously and perhaps have led to a fight.

Despite the prevalence of friendly insult, it is of course entirely possible that an insult which was intended to test and reinforce primary bonds may backfire or go too far and be misinterpreted by its recipient as a serious insult. In another example from my prep-school days, two friends of mine were top players on the football team, but had known each other a relatively short time. One tried to kid the other by insulting him and hiding his football helmet. This teasing was not intended as a malicious affront, but was interpreted as such by the offended boy, who reacted by punching the jokester and breaking his nose. In this instance, the object of an intended joke evidently felt that his incipient friendship with the teaser was not strong enough at that point to justify defining the action as just kidding. Thus, any kind of kidding or nonmaliciously intended insult behavior, even among close friends, may well backfire, with an effect opposite to that which the offender intended. Moreover, as the previous examples show, there is a close relationship between insult and humor. An act or remark with a derogatory content may either be taken seriously, or regarded as an attempt at humor. If the insulter and the object of his affront are close enough friends so that the insult is regarded as humorous, the insult ironically becomes a means of reasserting the strength of the primary relationship between them. If, however, the offender is a complete stranger, or is not a close friend of the insulted person, there is much less chance that an insult will be considered just kidding. In most instances, the offended person has the choice of how he wishes to define the situation: he may take serious offense, or he may simply laugh it off. In any event, there is often a thin line between humor and insult; in some instances, an act or remark intended as a joke will be defined by its object as a serious affront and may well lead to an angry response.

Another example of the way in which an intended bit of humor was defined as a serious insult involves a practical joke once played upon Andrew Jackson while he was still a senator. Jackson had no formal legal training and consequently made a practice, while speaking in the Senate, of continually referring to a legal text by a Professor Bacon. One of his colleagues, amused by Jackson's habitual reliance upon this tome, had a package delivered to Jackson with the inscription "In hopes that this will prove edifying to your legal exercises." Inside the elaborately wrapped package was a large slab of bacon. Jackson, very sensitive about his lack of formal training and temperamentally quite touchy, was infuriated and was dissuaded from challenging the jokester to a duel only when mutual friends intervened. In this instance, the humor obviously backfired [Kane, 1951:286].

Thus, despite the sense of comradeship and primary group solidarity which the bantering about of nonserious insults among friends may engender, as among Smith's group of firemen, there is always the danger than an affectionate affront or a practical joke will be defined by its receiver as a serious insult. Another possibility is that the object of a humorously insulting act or remark will define the joke as in bad taste, a kind of middle ground between humor and serious insult. A case in point involved an interaction between an ethnographer and a native woman in Turkey whom he had come to know in the course of studying her society. In the Turkish village he was studying, Makal found that it was a common practice for the women and girls to scatter over the roads where the oxen were driven to gather up the animal droppings to use as fertilizer:

It was just the time when the oxen were wandering through the village. I found the women following the cows and picking up the droppings in handfuls. There was one white-haired woman who had rolled up her sleeves and was carrying a huge ball of dung in her arms. I called out as a joke, "Hello Granny! What's that?"

The old woman recognized Makal's voice and, instead of accepting the facetious question as a joke, took offense because she thought he was making fun of her. She got quite angry, and cried out to the would-be comedian:

"Go away! This is no time for joking. You seem to be in good spirits. All right! Some people work hard and some eat well, eh? If you were in our place, you'd collect dung just as readily" [Makal, 1954:78-79].

Makal regretted his attempt at humor, since he realized on the basis of the woman's response that he had unintentionally hurt her feelings. This incident exemplifies the thin line that separates humor both from bad taste and actual insult; in most cases, it is how the recipient chooses to define the act or remark, rather than the intent of the perpetrator, which determines its outcome. There are many instances, also in a wide variety of cultures, in which a would-be humorist may not be conscious of the effect that his actions or words have. This is particularly true in instances of teasing: the teaser may feel that he is just kidding around, yet his words or actions may be perceived in an entirely different light by those who are the butt of his humor. In his account of the family behavior patterns of the Tewa Indians, Whitman remarks that joking and teasing among parents and children often takes a "quietly malicious turn" [Whitman, 1947:56]. As he describes such parent-child teasing, the parent may take something from a child and pretend not to give it back. The parent and the victim both ostensibly regard such behavior as a joke, but the child nearly always shows signs of insecurity and tension while the joke lasts. Moreover, such teasing (among the Tewa as among parents and children of many other cultures) is dependent upon the primary relationship that exists between them; if a stranger were to tease the child in a similar fashion, the parents would take offense. Whitman's examination of the ambiguous character of parent-child teasing, together with its dependency upon the primary relationship, is based upon observation of family life within a primitive society, but no doubt the same characteristics of teasing and joking can be found in the family behavior patterns of more complex societies. Even though a primary relationship may exist between an offender and his victim, and even though both may define a derogatory or teasing act or remark as a joke, the object of the joke may experience negative subjective effects. An advice column in the *Dayton Journal Herald* (April 19, 1974) exemplifies the inherent risk which is involved in the use of insult as a show of affection. A seventeen-year-old girl wrote complaining about her two best friends, who had begun

to make wisecracks about me, sometimes to my face and even more behind my back.

My other friends don't think this is a serious problem. They're just being funny, they say. Or they suggest I just make wisecracks back.

Ellen, I am miserable about my two former friends and do not look at this as a joking matter. I am so upset. It seems that even when I read sometimes, I am thinking about their cruel remarks instead of concentrating on my lessons.

My whole life is becoming a "downer." What would you suggest?

Ellen's reply:

Cruel remarks are a witless excuse for "humor." But there's no reason you can't use your own wits as a weapon against them. If your former friends put you down in front of others, a remark such as "Is something in your diet making you disagreeable lately?" or "Did you get up on the wrong side of the bed this morning?" may make them realize that their insulting remarks are inappropriate.

If they insult you privately, use any opportunity when others aren't around to ask them frankly what has caused their change of attitude.

I hope that you get some answers. But first, it's necessary to speak up, rather than suffer in silence.

In a wide variety of cultures, humor serves both as a means of affirming friendship and of expressing derision, of testing and strengthening primary bonds and breaking them. If insult-related humor has aggressive potentiality, it stands to reason that sociocultural systems should have developed ways of controlling the possibility that it might be dysfunctional to the system. Let us now compare some of the various institutionalized means of controlling the potentially destructive expression of insult-related humor.

The Joking Relationship in Primitive Societies

Because of the precariousness of many kinds of relationships involving the possibility of aggressive humor, many primitive societies have attempted to alleviate the tensions inherent in certain kinds of relationships (such as between siblings-in-law, because of their conflicting kinship obligations) by providing a semi-institutionalized pattern known as the "joking relationship." In many tribal and village sociocultural systems, the joking relationship exists between occupants of kinship categories whose competitive claims to hereditary rights are likely to give rise to open conflict. Among the Mossi tribespeople of West Africa, for example, the joking relationship is a structured part of the formally defined relationships between both siblings and siblings-in-law. Joking among the Mossi of different yet marriage-tied kinship groups serves to create a sense of primary bonding between the groups because it serves to reduce tension in a situation of potential conflict [Hammond, 1964:261]. This conflict-avoidance function is also the basis of the pattern of joking relationships among masters and slaves, such as that found among the West African

Hausa tribe. According to Smith, joking relationships between Hausa owners and slaves served to relieve some of the tensions inherent in their interactions [Smith, 1955:45]. Among the Yao of Southeast Asia, the joking relationship exists between both the headman and his villagers, and between the cross-cousins of different matrilineage and patrilineage groups. As in the African tribal societies, the Yao joking relationships serve to dissipate the hostility between both the dominant headman and his subjects, and between competing subgroups, so that harmony in the village is maintained [Mitchell, 1956:203].

Thus the joking relationship is not only a semi-institutionalized characteristic of a number of widely separate primitive sociocultural systems, but performs similar functions in every social system in which it is found. Moreover, joking relationships are evidently a quite successful means of achieving peace and stability among individuals and subgroups with competing interests. In his discussion of the joking relationships between the various subgroups that comprise the Hausa tribal structure, Smith points out that such relationships are "said to have been accompanied by a permanent peace; they were regarded as the expression of linkages between . . . groups which stabilized the wider framework within which the Seven Hausa States maintained their existence. . . ." The joking relationship thus appears to provide a viable means of reconciling and counteracting the tensions of a social relationship between two or more groups that are structurally divided from each other to the point of having potentially competitive interests likely to lead to conflict, but at the same time bound to each other by strong ties (such as marriage). The joking relationship between such groups deflects the undercurrent of hostility and mutual wariness, thus heading off open conflict between them.

8

SOCIALIZATION THROUGH INSULT

Insult is one type of negative response, but only in the limited sense of expressing a critical, nonaccepting evaluation of whatever behavior the object of the response is engaged in. In a functional sense, negative response, including insult, performs many positive functions for the maintenance of sociocultural systems. One of the most significant of these is the role of insult in the socialization process. Social and task learning takes place in part through positive and negative response directed at the learner's performance so that the culturally correct patterns of behavior might be inculcated. Insult is one type of response that expresses severe disapproval. Insult is a more severe form of response because it not only involves a negative evaluation of a learner's performance, but also tends to cast aspersions upon the individual's abilities in general. Thus, unlike mere criticism, insult as a type of negative response cuts deeper, aiming to create a sense of shame and anger so as, in the ideal-typical situation, to motivate the learner to establish behavior patterns congruent with the socializer's expectations of the sociocultural system that the socializer represents. Let us examine the role of insult as a socialization mechanism in tribal and village societies and then determine whether similar patterns exist in the socialization processes of modern industrialized societies.

Socialization and Insult in the Tribal-Village Context

In most tribal and village societies, boys undergo a rite of passage which marks their entry into manhood. In most cultures puberty rites, particularly (though not exclusively) those for males, are a time of trial in which the boy must show his worthiness to be considered a man. The years previous to his full acceptance as an adult are often filled with humiliation and insult directed at him by the community. The preinitiate in many tribal and village societies occupies a low social position in which he is subjected to various kinds of insult. In the Lau tribal culture, for example, the boy from approximately age seven to the time of his initiation (between eight and thirteen) lives a very humiliating existence. He is ignored, teased, tormented, insulted, and overworked. He is referred to as a *pilo*, a degrading, humorously insulting term with obscene connotations. The status of the pilo is very marginal; he is neither a child nor a man. He is no longer allowed to play with children in mixed groups, but he is also barred from taking part in the men's work or men's pleasures. As a result, the pilo develops a sense of inferiority which is exacerbated by young men and initiated youths who mock and insult him continuously for their amusement. The humiliation and insult that the pilo suffers, even though they constitute negative response, nonetheless have definite functions for the Lau socialization process. Because of his hatred of the pilo status, the boy becomes strongly motivated to learn and develop manly behavior patterns and to undergo the rigors of formal initiation so as to escape the degradation of being a lowly preinitiate [Thompson, 1940:44].

Closely related to the low status of the preinitiate is the fact that in many tribal and village societies, it is a grave insult to call anyone a "boy." Among the Kogi tribesmen, for example, "You look like a boy" is the gravest insult which can be uttered. It is an insult which produces deep emotions of anger and resentment in the particular Kogi who is offended in this manner. In Kogi society, as in many other similar contexts, the preinitiate is not only held in low esteem but is seen as a threat because he does not know and hence is not able to observe the rules of conduct of the men. The boy is thus an asocial element who poses a danger to the society in much the same way that a deviant is regarded as dangerous to many people in modern industrialized societies. Accordingly, like deviants in other cultures, the preinitiates of the Kogi tribe are not only insulted, but are used as scapegoats for the misfortunes that befall the tribe. When something goes wrong, it is the "boys'" fault [Reichel-Dolmatoff, 1951:212].

Thus, it is no wonder that the puberty rites of tribal and village societies are invested with a great deal of significance, both for the young men who are being initiated and for the society as a whole. It is impossible to overemphasize the importance that the initiation ritual has for those who are undergoing it. The rite of passage marks the time when the boy is no longer to be subjected to the continual degradation and insult of being treated as a nonperson.

The full significance of the initiation ritual of a typical tribal society is afforded in the anthropologist Henry's account of the puberty rites of the Bambara, which are essentially similar for both boys and girls. In Bambara society, circumcision is the central symbolic focus of the puberty rite. Girls as well as boys are circumcised, the former by means of a clitoral excision. During the ceremonies, the Bambara chief reminds everyone of the significance of the event, particularly the new status that is confirmed with circumcision:

"Yes!" the chief exclaims, "our newly circumcised children are on the path of their fathers; they are now Bambara! . . . they can henceforth take part in our games, our merrymaking, and our rites. May everyone know it and no one forget, or ever treat them as if they were uncircumcised—that is the deepest insult!"

At the end of the ceremony, the headman proclaims the end of the initiatory period, recalls its principal events, and indicates by name which specific boys and girls have participated in the rite. He again emphasizes that there is no worse insult among the Bambara than to treat a Bambara as uncircumcised. Again, this shows the central importance of insult in the Bambara, the Kogi, and other tribal societies' socialization processes. The preinitiate who has not yet learned (and hence does not practice) the behavior patterns and values of adults is treated with contempt and is continually insulted so that he or she will be motivated to conform to the required patterns, undergo initiation, and therefore escape the insult of the lowly preinitiate. In this way, the individual contributes to the maintenance of the sociocultural patterns of his tribe. Most significantly for the tribal society as a whole, the insults directed against the not-fully-socialized member constitute a prime mechanism for the continuation of the sociocultural system of the tribe [Monteil, 1924:270].

Among the Bambara, as we have seen, the rite of passage is the same for both boys and girls. But in some other tribal and village cultures, there is a substantial differentiation between the sexes in the behavioral patterns they are required to evince and the ideals they are encouraged to emulate. Generally speaking, the sexual differentiation related to initiation is greater in patriarchal societies, and becomes extreme in most caste and estate systems, a point that we shall emphasize later in this chapter. But in terms of tribal-village norms of initiation, there are many examples of sex-specific values which are emphasized for the different sexes. For girls, the most common value that the initiate is required to embody is that of physical beauty. Thus for the South American La Guajiro Indians the most important requirement for the girl initiate is that she do her utmost to embody the ideals of beauty held by the culture. Accordingly, the girl initiate may not scratch any part of her body, because that might leave visible scars that could detract from her beauty. Girls who have physical defects are subjected to insults and humiliation [Pineda Giraldo, 1950:52].

Perhaps the most common sex-specific socialization patterns found in all kinds of societies are those that emphasize for the male tribal member the development of toughness, physical endurance, courage, and other traits related to fighting ability and military prowess. And in tribal-village, caste-estate, and modern societies alike, insult serves as a major mechanism whereby military values are internalized and fighting abilities are developed. Within the three major types of social systems, there are many cultural differentiations; nonetheless, the basic similarities to be found between many otherwise widely divergent cultures are quite striking. These similarities in the manner in which military abilities are inculcated suggest that even in widely different societies it is necessary for collective survival that males develop military prowess. Early and constant training of such a nature is often necessary for the welfare and survival of a society. What does such training involve in different kinds of societies and cultures?

Among the Maori of New Zealand, boys begin at a very early age to practice the use of weapons, at first with such harmless objects as reeds, with which they practice the rudiments of spear fighting. As the boys become older, they are taught by older men how to use various weapons and how to parry and avoid the weapons of opponents. Such skills are important to the Maori, but perhaps the values that the young men internalize, largely through the direction of severe and humiliating insults against boys who fail to display military skills, are even more important. As in other kinds of societies, the most severe insults among the Maori are reserved for those members of a tribe who fail to fulfill their military duties [Best, 1924:80-82].

Among Creek Indian youths, those who are passive and have seldom taken part in wars and are thus not militarily distinguished are called "old women," the greatest term of reproach that can be used against a Creek. In addition, those who have not distinguished themselves in warfare are liable to be insulted by a common slur: "You are nobody!" Among the Creeks, this is a very offensive expression and is used cautiously [Swanton, 1924-25:427]. Thus, among the Creeks as among many other peoples, social status depends on military prowess.

Similar relationships between male socialization, military values, and insult can be found in many caste and estate societies, particularly those in which the highest class constitutes the military elite. Indeed, the entire upper-class value systems of such groups as the Prussian Junkers revolved around the emphasis upon militarism. The Junker from his earliest youth internalized not only a sense of his own innate superiority, but the necessity and obligation to defend his honor. Closely related to this was the military training that the young male Junker received from his tenderest years. His parents continually stressed the militaristic values and virtues of his culture [Martin, 1945:40].

Modern Military Socialization and Insult

Insults that are directed toward nonaggressive individuals and pre-initiates in tribal-village and caste-estate societies are also found in the training programs of military institutions of modern societies. In lieu of a formalized puberty rite for males in most modern societies, the basic training period—with its stress upon the development of endurance and fighting abilities and its pervasive use of insult against those who fail to conform to the aggressive model—constitutes a functional equivalent of the formal rite of passage of the tribal-village and some caste-estate societies.

Just as the preinitiate in many tribes is subjected to constant insult and ridicule and has, at best, a marginal social status, the modern military recruit is the object of a virtual barrage of insults. Studies of military socialization in modern societies have shown that insult is one of a number of socializing mechanisms that help break down the recruit's previous bases of identity so that he will be motivated to conform to the norms and embody the values of the military organization. The overall patterns of insult in the military training programs are basically similar to the ridicule to which tribal preinitiates are subjected. In both the modern and the tribal contexts, the humiliation that is engendered by severe and continual insults motivates the initiate to escape his lowly status by conforming to the expectations that are forcefully imposed upon him. In addition, the recruit is prevented from having any sources of positive reinforcement other than for behavior which conforms to the values and expectations of the military organization. Thus, the insults he receives tear down his premilitary sources of self-esteem and replace them with a positive self-regard that results from his developing capacities to embody military virtues and display fighting prowess.

Examples of the role of insult in military socialization can be found in nearly any account of the basic training process. The U. S. Marine Corps, in particular, is well known for the verbal abuse it gives its recruits as a part of the training process. The following are examples of the use of insult in the Marine boot camp, involving an exchange between a recruit named Adamczyk and a drill instructor. In this dialogue, it is interesting to note the vehement way in which the basic symbol of the recruit's previous identity—his name—is forcibly denied and replaced by an insulting substitute:

"Up and out! Let's go!" shouted the D. I. "Hey you, carrot-top! You'd best move before I put a boot up your skinny young ass. Up! You got a name, maggot?" yelled the D. I.

"Adamczyk, sir. Thomas S., sir."

"You do situps like elephant shits, maggot, slow and sloppy. From now on that's your name—Shit. Understand?"

"Yes, sir."

"Now, let's hear it. And it had best come right from your gut."

"Sir, my name is Thomas S. Adamczyk, sir!"

"Your old lady's ass it is! Didn't your drill instructor just tell you your name is Shit? You can't do pushups right, you can't say 'sir' right, and now you can't even remember your own name." Maguire [the D. I.] stuck his face close to Adamczyk's, ... [who] stared straight ahead. "From now on, maggot, your name is Doubleshit, you got that?" [Flanagan, 1971:9-10].

The military is by no means the only context in which socialization-related insults are common. In adolescent peer groups insult is often a means whereby the status configurations of the group are established and hence serves a positive function for the group as a whole.

Hazing, Sounding, and Slashing: Insult and the Peer Group

In the military systems of modern societies, hazing is an accepted part of the basic training process. In nonmilitary contexts such as college fraternities, however, hazing has in recent years been frowned upon because of the tragic events that have occasionally occurred: a number of fraternity initiates have suffered serious injury or death as a result of the pranks that have been pulled on them or the humiliating stunts they have had to perform as a part of fraternal initiation procedures.

Hazing can be differentiated from other forms of adolescent peer-group insult behavior in that the former usually is related to the socialization of neophytes into a more or less formalized organization such as a college fraternity or a school. Just as in the military context, the hazing process employs insult as a means of emphasizing the inferior status of the pre-initiate. In any group, particularly small groups, new individuals who seek membership constitute a threat to the existing status patterns within the group. Since the new individual has no clear status within the group at first, the group is not sure where to place him in the status order. As the most expedient solution to this problem, and in order to minimize the status threat that neophytes pose, many groups relegate new individuals to a position of low status and reinforce this lowly position through formal or informal humiliation and insults. A good example of this is the typical treatment given a number of freshman students in a military academy. The following is from a film version of Calder Willingham's novel of the effects of hazing in a Southern military academy. In the scene, freshmen are ordered into the room of two upperclassmen, who force the new students to stand at attention while they are subjected to a rain of insults:

Ain't no hope for you guys, no how. I want to see two powerful little chests up in the air!

What a creep. What a fantastic creep. My, my, what a creep.

Sorry looking specimen, ain't he?   Don't look like much of nothin'
to me. An idiot like that is better off dead.

What are you laughing at? You're a freshman around here and don't
you forget it!

Although hazing has been officially prohibited by most college
authorities, the practice still is carried on sub rosa in many fraternities.
The preinitiate pledge occupies a low social position and is continually
reminded that he is not a fully accepted member of the fraternity. He is
forced to carry out humiliating tasks and is the target of both overt and
subtle insults directed at him by the actives as part of becoming socialized
into the fraternity. This basic pattern is, in essence, quite similar to the
treatment of preinitiates in many tribal societies. In the tribal, modern
military, and fraternity contexts, insult is a prime mechanism of socialization in that it emphasizes and reinforces the low status of the neophyte
and motivates him to adopt the values and behavioral expectations of the
group.

Insult is also a significant aspect of interaction among members of less
formalized groups such as adolescent street corner gangs or similar
informal peer groups. A prime example is the practice of "sounding"
(also known as "doing the dozens," "ranking," and a variety of other
terms depending on the locality), a form of insult behavior common
among black ghetto youths, particularly delinquents. But its basic
patterns are also found among middle- and upper-class youths in essentially
similar insult games. As an insult game, sounding often is characterized by
certain ritualistic qualities (as in the elaborate rhymed insults of some
"sounders"), but it is not institutionalized or formalized in a strict sense
and arises entirely spontaneously in the course of peer-group interaction.
And although sounding occasionally leads to overt violence, violence is
a normatively disapproved response to a sounding insult since it constitutes an admission by the insulted boy of his failure to put down the
other through the exercise of verbal skills.

Sounding clearly exhibits the close relationship between insult and
humor which we have discussed previously. Sounding usually involves
two actors, but it takes place before a peer-group audience, and thus
serves as an important source of amusement for the group. Most studies
of sounding observe that the individual sounder who manages to elicit the
most laughter from the group is tacitly regarded as the winner of the
verbal duel. The presence of the group also serves to define the insults as

humorous rather than serious; hence, "The presence of a group seems to be especially important in controlling the game. Without the control of the group, sounding will often lead to a fight" [Dollard, 1939:5].

Underlying the humorous content of sounding insults are deep-seated anxieties, particularly relating to the adolescent's sense of masculine identity and the black youth's internalized sense of social inferiority. This is illustrated by the following "one-liners" collected from black ghetto youths in Chicago:

Your family is so poor, the rats and roaches eat lunch out.

I walked into your house and your family was running around the table. I said, "Why you doin' that?" Your Mama say, "First one drops, we eat."

Yo Mama is so bowlegged, she looks like the bit of a donut.

Your house is so small the roaches walk single file.

Yo Mama sent her picture to the lonely hearts club, and they sent it back and said, "We ain't that lonely!" [Kochman, 1969:31-33].

While these insults may elicit appreciative laughter from the peer group, such humor also serves as a release of deep-seated anxieties and hostilities arising from the black youth's recognition of his environmental and familial disadvantages. Thus, sounding has been linked to the overall psychosocial growth of the black male: a single round of a dozen or so exchanges frees a great deal of pent-up aggression.

Such aggressions arise primarily from the social-environmental and social-structural inferiorities inflicted upon the black ghetto youth. What about the "deeper" facets of personality development involving masculine identity and social acceptability as a member of a group of peers? In this sense, according to Matza's analysis, "Sounding is a probing of one's depth, taking the form of insult. One's depth is never definitively certified. It is sounded almost daily. Most sounding is a probing of one's manliness and one's membership. Are you really a man, or just a kid? Are you really one of us, or just faking it?"

The adolescent, particularly the black ghetto youth who has little socio-cultural support from a society which seeks to develop in him a sense of inferiority, experiences substantial uncertainties as to his own masculine identity and acceptability. Through sounding and by learning the verbal skills necessary to respond effectively to insult, the youth is able to deal with these anxieties within the context of his peer group. Sounding functions as a means of dealing with adolescent anxieties in a manner which avoids the direct questions of an individual's status and basic worth, but nevertheless enables a youth to deal with his anxieties by obtaining the reactions of what Mead would term his "significant others." In the practice of sounding, "one can anticipate the following kinds of responses [to direct questions] ":

Do I really like you? Yea, come here and suck and I'll show you how much I like you.

Are you really a man? Well, I don't know, man; sometimes I think you a kid and sometimes you a fag.

The anticipation of these sorts of responses makes good sense, as one excellent way of temporarily alleviating one's own anxiety is the invidious derogation of others. Sounding is both a source of anxiety and a vehicle by which it may be temporarily alleviated [Matza, 1964:53-54].

Insult games are by no means characteristic of only lower-status youth. "Slashing" is the term applied to insult behavior among the students at a largely upper-class, white male preparatory school which I attended from 1957 to 1961. The following descriptions of these insult games are based on my recollections of student experiences at the school and thus are not scientifically adequate. My purpose here is to provide the basis for a more adequate study of insult behavior among male adolescents of the upper-middle and upper classes, through an observational and interview study. My recollections are offered in lieu of such a study.

Slashing may be compared to the practice of hazing, common in military academies, fraternities, and other male student groups, characterized by exclusionism and by traditionalist-conservative values. Slashing is different from hazing in two basic ways. First, slashing was largely an informal activity that could take place between any students. Furthermore, it occurred in an entirely spontaneous manner. Hazing, on the other hand, is semiritualized and usually is inflicted by upperclassmen upon underclassmen as a part of the initiation process. Second, hazing may be functionally analyzed as serving to minimize the threat to existing status relationships posed by new additions to a group. By semiritually subjecting novices to various forms of humiliation, hazing protects the group against a disruption of the existing status configurations among its members, at the same time reaffirming and socializing basic group norms and values. In contrast, slashing served mainly to define and establish status relationships among the students at the school. In other words, slashing was the primary means by which the student pecking order was established and maintained.

In its overt manifestations slashing consisted of insinuating in various ways that an individual was unintelligent, unathletic, or of low class. The content of the "slashes" corresponded generally with the manifest values of the school, which stressed athletics, scholarship, and class-manners. For example, a very common type of slash consisted of the term "Duh!" mouthed in a sneering, mocking manner. This, of course, was meant to insinuate that the object of the insult was stupid. In reply, the recipient would usually say something like "You're not too cool either, Smith," or some similar retort. "Coolness" was a salient, "latent" (i.e., not formally legitimated) value among the students. It may be defined as a kind of combination of athletic appearance and masculine mannerisms. The students who were the most "cool" had the highest status, and were largely immune from slashing. Those who were not "cool" tended to be low on the pecking order. For example, if the particular individual did not have athletic ability, he would be slashed either by being called "spaz" (short for "spastic") or by mocking his manner of walking, his characteristic mannerisms, or both. At times slashing could become quite cruel. One student who was at the school during my freshman year was a very friendly fellow who, as a child, had had an operation on his leg in which part of his calf muscle had been removed, causing him to walk in a very awkward manner. Several times he was subjected to slashing in which a student would walk alongside him, mocking his mode of walking and taunting him with mock friendliness. Despite pathetic efforts to gain acceptance, the semicrippled student spent a miserable year at the bottom of the pecking order and left the next year.

Responses to slashing were dependent, of course, on personality factors. Some individuals chose to counterinsult, and often long, drawn-out slashing "duels" would occur. Occasionally, these "duels" would take on a semipublic character, similar to the sounding among black ghetto youth. A familiar topic of discussion at the dining table would involve Smith and Jones who had "really slashed each other" the previous evening.

Slashing may or may not be an example of more general teasing behavior that occurs among children and adolescents. At any rate, the parallels between slashing and sounding suggest that insult behavior may not be peculiar to lower-status adolescent groups. It is interesting to note that the subject matter of both sounding and slashing (in terms of the manifest content of the insults) refers clearly to the values of the differing milieux. This suggests that insult behavior may be a general mechanism of peer-group socialization among adolescents, functioning both to establish status relationships within peer groups and to enable the adolescent to deal with the anxieties of masculine identity and the values of manliness that are imposed upon him and which he must attempt in some way to embody. This problem is particularly acute in modern societies, which, for the most part, lack any definite initiation rite that affords the tribal-village youth a clear-cut definition of his adult status.

9

INSULT AND THE POLITICAL PROCESS

Insult and Democracy

Insult plays an important role in the democratic political process. One very significant aspect of political insult is its support of the democratic system. Freedom to insult one's political opponents is an indispensable democratic privilege. Under totalitarian and autocratic regimes, insults against political leaders are anything but lightly regarded; those who engage in them publicly and are caught are usually imprisoned, if not murdered.

Indeed, any criticism of totalitarian political leaders is regarded as treasonous, even if it does not necessarily involve insult: witness the very strong reaction of the Soviet regime against such critics. In a democratic system, however, politically related insult is not only accepted—it is a basic way of expressing political beliefs and belittling political opponents. In America, insult behavior is manifest in a number of ways: as one technique of politicians and their supporters who seek to discredit opponents; as a tool of political argument between those of conflicting political beliefs; and as a tool preventing holders of political office from developing a too exalted view of themselves. In a democratic system, incumbents are always open to abuse by even their most humble constituents and are constantly being insulted (and therefore kept in check) by those who do not completely approve of their policies or their performance.

In the competition between political candidates in a democratic system, an important method of asserting one's suitability for office is to maintain that one's opponent is not qualified. Sometimes, though not always, a candidate's criticisms of his opponent's qualifications take on an insulting aspect—rare is the candidate whose campaign avoids derogatory references to his opponent that verge on insult. In many political contests, in fact, it is quite common for a candidate to base his entire campaign not upon his own merits, but upon his opponent's alleged shortcomings. It is only a short step from such depreciation and derogation to actual insult between opponents.

One of the first steps that a person who goes into political life in a democratic society must take is to ensure that there is nothing in his past life or present situation which could be used against him by opponents who are looking for some basis upon which to undermine his character or his personal reputation. For example, much political capital was made of the extramarital affairs of Grover Cleveland and Warren G. Harding. A popular ditty at the time of Cleveland's campaign was:

> Ma, Ma, where is Pa?
> Gone to the White House, Ha, Ha, Ha.

Aside from alleged moral ineptitudes, American politicians' physical features have always provided subject matter for abuse. We think of Abraham Lincoln as a dignified even mythic figure, but in his own time his gaunt physique and unattractive features were the subject of countless insults by political cartoonists and numerous others who did their best to portray him not only as monumentally ugly, but also as an uncouth, unlettered bumpkin completely lacking in any of the physical and social graces. In our own time, political cartoonists continue to caricature political figures. Although such efforts might appear humorous to some, the subjects of their drawings do not always take them as lightly. For example, during an interview soon after he had been elected for a second presidential term, Richard Nixon referred to the work of Herblock, a political cartoonist, who has for many years portrayed Nixon as a grotesque figure with a long, shovel-like nose. Nixon commented on the necessity for the politician to remain personally unaffected not only by such graphic insults, but also by the myriad other kinds of abuse inevitably thrown at him:

"The major weakness of inexperienced people," the President said, "is that they take things personally, especially in politics, and that can destroy you.

"Years ago when I was a young Congressman, things got under my skin. Herblock the cartoonist got to me. But now when I walk into this office I am cool and calm."

Of course the significant point in Nixon's remarks was that he overcame his sensitivity to political insults by simply withdrawing from the possibility of any exposure to them:

"I could go up the wall watching TV commentators. I don't. I get my news summary the staff prepares every day and it's great; it gives all sides.

"I never watch TV commentators or the news shows when they are about me. That's because I don't want decisions influenced by personal emotional reaction. . . .

"I never allow myself to get emotional. Now, there are Congressmen and Senators who cut me up—Fulbright, for example—but when he comes here, we're the best of friends, at least I feel I am" [Pett, 1973:38].

The danger of this isolation from insult, of course, is that once a politician becomes powerful enough to do so, he may well insulate himself against abuse and hence undermine the central function of political insult: to provide a check to those in power who may be tempted to think of themselves in grandiose terms, above the rest of humanity and hence not subject to insults. When a political leader deliberately insulates himself against possible insults, he undercuts a basic informal process of the democratic system.

Congressional Conflict and the Calumnies of Constituents

Presidents, of course, are not the only political figures subjected to insult as part and parcel of the democratic process. The floors of both the House and the Senate have often been the scene of political debate shading over into personal abuse. During the earlier part of the last century, insults and counterinsults were very common among senatorial and congressional foes. As a result, many duels were fought. The duel between Aaron Burr and Alexander Hamilton, for example, arose out of political conflicts—specifically from some derogatory remarks made by

Hamilton which were interpreted by Burr as implying that he was "deficient in integrity, honor, or any other quality requisite to the character of a gentleman." As discussed in a previous chapter, duelling as a practice was prevalent primarily in the aristocratic South; its occurrence among northern politicians such as Burr and Hamilton can be attributed to the influence of aristocratic culture and values which lingered into the early part of the nineteenth century, particularly among "gentlemen" of the upper classes—which senators and congressmen of the era undoubtedly considered themselves to be.

Far more common among politicians was the art of verbal combat, which for the greater part did not lead to violent responses, but which nonetheless gave rise to great and lasting enmities between political rivals and those of contradictory views. One notable practitioner of the art was Thaddeus Stevens, often described as a "fiery" opponent of slavery. Most of Stevens's fire took the shape of insults directed against his senate colleagues who supported slavery. Stevens's fight against slavery is a case study in the use of insult against political opponents; his insults, sometimes eloquent, were often merely gross. He continually referred to slavery advocates as "fools and blackguards," and often tinged his abuse with sharp wit. For example, a political enemy once met Stevens on a narrow path and stated, "I never step aside for a skunk!" whereupon Stevens, moving out of the way, replied, "But I always do." In reply to a diatribe against him by Representative Thomas Ross, who was the leading supporter of slavery in the antebellum era, Stevens gave a typically devastating reply:

> There is, in the natural world, a little, spotted, contemptible animal which is armed with a fetid, volatile, penetrating virus, which so pollutes whoever attacks it as to make him offensive to himself and all around him for a long time. Indeed, he is almost incapable of purification. Nothing, sir, no insult shall provoke me to crush so filthy a beast!

Stevens's insults were by no means limited to comparing his opponents to skunks. In response to President Andrew Johnson's having publicly called Stevens a traitor for advocating a strongly pro-black reconstruction program, Stevens replied that Johnson was a "knave and a fool." When one congressman tried to point out that Johnson, like Stevens, was a "self-made man," Stevens snapped back, "Glad to hear it. It relieves God Almighty of the responsibility." According to many historians, Stevens's uncompromising support of blacks and the rights of the "common man" was an important factor in the early fight for black freedom and black rights, such as they were at the time. Had it not been for Stevens's use of devastating insult as a potent political weapon, it is likely that the plight of the black man would have been even worse than it was, particularly after the Civil War. He was perhaps the pre-eminent egalitarian and anti-racist of his time. (Morrill, 1971)

Insults in Contemporary Congressional Politics

Today, the political officeholder must be ready both to receive and to give abuse, not only from and to his political opponents, but his constituents as well. Stephen Young, a recent senator from Ohio, tells of some of the abuse he has received from certain constituents, particularly those on the political right who objected to his liberal stands. Unlike some of his colleagues, Young began composing one-line answers to insulting letters soon after he took office. His rationale was that "every man has the right to answer back when he is being bullied. And so, when some wiseacre challenges my sincerity or patriotism, I let him have it." Here are some examples of the epistolary insults that Young received, and his counterinsult replies:

A fellow in Cincinnati sent me a long tirade about my behavior in Congress and out of it. He went on and on. I answered him:
"No, I don't believe I have long furry ears; I do thank you, however, for your gentlemanly manner of calling me a Jackass."
There was really nothing to tell the man from South Euclid who said I was the sort of fellow who would enjoy desecrating the graves in Arlington Cemetery except:
"Sir: You are a liar."
I tried to stop myself, but ended up by telling an overwrought minister:
"As one Methodist to another may I suggest that you concentrate on preaching the Gospel instead of insulting a public servant."

To another constituent who had criticized Young's stand against the Ultra-Right and asked "Who do you represent?" Young wrote back: "Buster, I know I don't represent a pipsqueak like you." To a Cincinnati woman who wrote Young that he was "an old reprobate and a disgrace to the state of Ohio," Young countered: "Lady, reading your abusive, insulting and untruthful letter causes me to feel happy that I am not your husband." In reply to many insulting letters, Young would send a standard reply: "Some crackpot sent me a letter to which your name was affixed."

Such give-and-take is part and parcel of the democratic political system. But instead of taking the abuse personally or attempting to insulate himself from it (as he could easily have done through his staff), Young commendably reacted in kind to the insults, thus asserting his views and exhibiting a certain kind of courage:

What would you say if you opened the morning mail and found a treasure like this:
"Buster, you represent the epitomy [sic] of pigsty thinking and cattle-type action. . . . Before you commence with your diurnal diarrhea of the mouth why do not for a change get the facts and attempt for once to make a truthful statement?"
I studied this masterpiece of English prose carefully and replied . . .
"I agree with Edmund Burke that there is a 'limit to which forebearance ceases to be a virtue'" [Young, 1964:87-98].

Nonetheless, Young points out that fewer than five or ten of the letters he receives each month are insulting or abusive. But that he, and every other politician, receives them, and that some (like Young) reply in kind says a lot about the nature of the democratic political system. In general, the prevalence of political insult and counterinsult is a kind of informal check upon any tendencies that an officeholder might have toward extreme self-aggrandizement, which could very easily lead to a complete lack of sensitivity to constituents' opinions other than those which support his views and stands. Moreover, that it is not only a legal, but a fairly common, practice to criticize politicians to the point of abusing and insulting them verbally is an often overlooked but vital distinction between democratic and authoritarian systems. In this sense, political insults can be viewed as functionally positive phenomena in that they are one means of maintaining and sustaining, as well as reflecting, the democratic process.

10

THE EDUCATIONAL USES OF INSULT

One of the ways in which learning takes place is through positive and negative response. In the ideal-typical learning situation, the educator wishes to instill some predetermined set of behavior patterns or knowledge. If the learner evinces the proper mode of behavior or a command of the material, he is rewarded; if he does not, he receives some form of negative response. Through a process of trial and error, he gradually learns to exhibit the expected modes of behavior or kinds of knowledge required of him. This model of the learning process is, of course, the classical conditioning model, and like all ideal-typical patterns, it is an oversimplification of the process that takes place in real life. Nonetheless, the centrality of the concept of response, particularly of the negative sort, in the conditioning model provides at least a starting point for our analysis of the role of insult in the educational process. As stated in the first chapter, insult is an extreme form of negative response. Insult goes beyond mere criticism because it imputes negative characteristics to the person as a whole, rather than merely to the particular behavior in which he is engaged. In other words, insult is a more encompassing type of negative response in that it fails to limit itself to a criticism of a particular behavior that a person is engaged in, going beyond so as to insinuate that the particular behavior is an indication of the general lack of worth of the person as a whole. As we have seen, insult is a central facet of the socialization process of most societies. The socializee is commonly of low social status and is often insulted and humiliated until he begins to exhibit the patterns of behavior that are expected of him. In educational institutions, such as our elementary and secondary schools, the use of insult and humiliation may not appear to be as blatant or severe as, for example, its ubiquitous use in military organizations. Humiliation and insult are, however, quite prevalent in modern educational institutions (including higher education) albeit appearing in more subtle ways. Let us examine some of the functions of insult in the educational process.

Vulnerability and Tyranny in the Classroom

In preparatory school I had a flinty Latin teacher who was so disdainful of students that during classes he never looked up from his book. After calling for different students to recite, he would listen to their efforts with undisguised contempt and, if the recitation were mediocre, would make some comment such as, "Well, Smith, you can always run a one-pump gas station," or "Well, there's always the New Mexico School of Road Repair." When the translation was particularly displeasing, he would insult the boy's father as well; there were so many alumni sons, and the teacher had been at the school so long, that he had taught many of the boys' fathers: "Well, Jones, your father wasn't much good either," was a typical remark. This rather blatant use of insult is perhaps more typical of the "traditionalist-conservative" (as the school styled itself) educational philosophy than of the more progressive educational ideologies, but nonetheless something like this Latin teacher's use of insult and humiliation in his teaching practices is found to some degree in most modern classrooms, although usually in more subtle forms. Even if insult and humiliation are not experienced as frequently by students in institutions more progressive than my prep school, nonetheless the threat of humiliation is a constant presence which serves as a powerful, if "informal," aspect of the educational process. And the power of such threat is related to the basic vulnerability of the student.

Jules Henry was one of the first scholars to call attention to the significance of vulnerability as a basic, if often unrecognized, trait that educational institutions create in their charges as one means of gaining and keeping power over them, as well as instilling in them a basic fear of failure that is necessary for them if they are to continue throughout their lives to be motivated to conform to the demands of their sociocultural milieu. In Henry's words:

It is . . . essential that society make men vulnerable. If a man is invulnerable society cannot reach him, and if society produces men who cannot be reached it cannot endure. . . .

To the end that man can be injured and thus brought to heel, an array of frightful devices has been created so that men will be meek and mild . . . in order for a society to survive it must create a vulnerable character structure in its member. . . .

The child's vulnerability is sustained and intensified by the elementary school, where he is at the teacher's mercy. The teacher . . . is the agent of vulnerability; and she transmits a sense of vulnerability through two weapons . . . discipline and the power to fail the child [Henry, 1971:9-24].

This educationally induced vulnerability extends beyond elementary school into high school and college. While supposedly imparting "knowledge," the teacher teaches the student to learn to conform to the expectations and to strive after the values set forth by his sociocultural context. Hence, as Henry puts it, the "fear of failure is the dark aspect of hope and striving for success."

Closely connected with its creation of a sense of vulnerability in its students is the school's latent function of selection. Beginning at the earliest preprimary and primary levels, schools are continually testing and evaluating students so as to determine who shall be allowed to become qualified for the professional and white-collar jobs and who shall be relegated to the vocational and trade occupations. Thus, both the threat and the actual use of humiliation and insult work in two basic ways. First, the teacher has it within his or her power to insult and humiliate those who do not conform to the required patterns. In more traditional contexts, such insult was fairly overt: the "stupid" child, for example, was required to wear a dunce cap, and thus became the object of insult and ridicule not only from the teacher but from his peers. Second, the child is exposed to the threat of a more structured kind of humiliation—poor grades and the possibility of being relegated to a "slow-learners" track or "general education" program, both of which carry with them the insulting stigma that the child is not "smart enough" to be in more "advanced" or "college-prep" classes.

In elementary schools, the insult and humiliation of being relegated to the "slow" basic classes, as opposed to the advanced sections, is very apparent in the responses of children and their parents, well shown in a film entitled *An Intellectual Caste System*, which describes the effects of the tracking system as employed in a suburban Atlanta elementary school system. Asked what they thought it meant to be in the three different tracks, students replied that being in an "advanced" course meant that one was "good" and "smart," while being in a "basic" class meant that a child was "bad" and "dumb." In a high school in Webster Groves, Missouri, students taking vocational courses were insultingly stigmatized as being "stupid" by the majority of students, who were enrolled in college preparatory courses. Thus in many schools, not only the subtle and not-so-subtle insults of teachers and peers, but also various selection mechanisms of the system work together to ensure that some students will be stigmatized and labelled as inferior, suitable only for menial and working-class jobs rather than for occupations requiring a college education. In this way, insult is one educational means whereby the stratification systems of societies are perpetuated.

Insult, Education, and the Perpetuation of the Vicious Circle

The use of insult to maintain the class structure of America is perhaps nowhere as clearly apparent as in the preponderance of insults directed against the lower-class child. As many scholars have pointed out, American elementary and secondary schools are oriented toward middle-class values and norms; thus, the schools operate largely on the basis of what Albert Cohen has termed the "middle-class measuring rod." For lower-class children, this means that their preschool socialization has been of little help, and in large measure may well have been a hindrance, in preparing them to cope with school expectations. As many studies have pointed out, the objective intelligence tests administered in schools are heavily weighted in favor of middle-class children because they test information and skills that the middle-class child is much more likely to have inculcated as part of his socialization within the family. More likely than not, the lower-class child is humiliated from his earliest days at school by being typed as a relatively incapable individual. Typically such children soon find themselves unable to do as well as their middle-class counterparts, and perhaps become the butt of insults both from fellow students and teachers that reinforce the idea that they are "dumb" or "stupid." Moreover, lower-class children may find that the clothes they wear, being less expensive than those of the middle-class students, will cause them to become the object of insults and ridicule.

All of these negative experiences of the lower-class child in the public school are, of course, intensified if the student also happens to be a member of a minority group. As Jonathan Kozol has dramatically recorded in his account of his experiences as a teacher in the Boston ghetto schools, black children are often viewed contemptuously by their white teachers, who often blatantly degrade and insult them. In a typical instance, Kozol describes the manner in which teachers accused black students of being liars without any proof. The typical teacher's attitude, according to Kozol, was that black children were basically liars, and hence the teachers felt no compunction in blatantly insulting their students. One incident to which Kozol refers specifically involved a substitute teacher who taught across the hall from him one afternoon. Kozol knew the students much better, of course, than did the substitute teacher. When corrected papers were handed back to the students by this middle-class white instructor, two of the black students did not receive theirs—their papers had obviously been lost in the shuffle that often accompanies the temporary shift to substitute teachers. The instructor automatically disbelieved their story, however, and, bringing them to the front of the classroom, so effectively disgraced and insulted them, that when she was finished even the two little black students believed that, somehow, they were liars [Kozol, 1967:56–57]. This example of the blatant use of insult against minority children in public is only one instance of the ubiquitous employment of such abuse, all of which serves the latent function of inculcating within such children a sense of their own inferiority, both intellectual and moral, and hence helping to perpetuate the socioeconomic order by denying to lower-class children successful educational experiences that could serve as the basis for social mobility. Calling elementary school children "liars" with no proof is, of course, only one of a large variety of insults to which lower-class and minority children are daily subject. Spanish-speaking children, as another example, are culturally and individually insulted by being punished for speaking Spanish at school, and are often diagnosed as subnormally intelligent on the basis of their performance on intelligence tests written in English.

On the secondary level, the selection and class-maintenance functions of the public school system become even more obvious, and insult plays an important role. As mentioned previously, lower-class and minority students are often relegated to the "general education" or vocational programs, which are typically underfunded. Moreover, students in such programs are looked down upon by the college-bound middle-class students. Teachers often deliberately insult lower-class and minority students by telling them, despite evidence to the contrary, that they do not have the ability to go to college and should be content with learning a trade or working in a factory. A most striking example of a teacher's use of blatant insult against a minority student is found in *The Autobiography of Malcolm X*. As a high school student, Malcolm had done quite well; his performance both scholastically and in extracurricular activities was sufficiently superior to allow him to dream of going to college to prepare for the legal profession. When he conveyed these ambitions to one of his favorite teachers, however, he was insultingly discouraged and told that he "should be realistic about being a nigger. A lawyer—that's no realistic goal for a nigger. You need to think about something you can be. You're good with your hands—making things. Why don't you plan on carpentry?" [Malcolm X, 1966:35–37].

The white teacher's discouragement, together with its insulting connotations, had a strong effect on Malcolm, particularly since he realized that the same teacher had encouraged many white students with scholastic records inferior to his to prepare for professional careers. This example shows very clearly the way in which teacher-student insult is an important mechanism whereby the public schools seek to maintain and sustain the existing class structure, first by deliberately internalizing a sense of inferiority in lower-class and minority students, and second by deliberately and insultingly discouraging their ambitions.

Having examined various functions of the use of insult within the elementary and secondary school contexts, let us now discuss the nature and functions of patterns of insult within higher education.

Insult in Higher Education

Academics are peculiarly prone to insulting one another, according to a commonly held conception of professional life. Backbiting between professional rivals both within the same disciplines and between different segments of the higher educational institution seems incongruous with the supposed commitment of academics to gentility and rationality. To what extent backbiting is peculiar to the academic profession is difficult to determine in any objective way; to my knowledge, there is no research effectively measuring the extent of insult among academics as compared with its manifestations in other professions. Without any undue assumptions about the degree of its ubiquity, then, let us assume that academic backbiting does exist and is fairly common, although not necessarily as common as popular conceptions would have us believe. Let us then look at some of its typical manifestations and attempt to analyze it as a particular form of insult behavior functionally related to the maintenance of the institutional framework in which it takes place. Again, as in all of our analyses of specific kinds of insult behavior, our focus will be upon the way in which the microcosm of interpersonal insults is related to the macrocosm of its sociocultural and institutional context.

Arthur Stinchcombe has written an interesting analysis of the social psychology underlying insults among academics. Pointing out that professors, since their earliest childhood, have typically enjoyed the status of the "brightest boy," he maintains that the uniqueness of this distinguishing status is threatened for the first time when the "brightest boy" becomes a professor. Most college students undergo this kind of readjustment in self-image when they find at the beginning of their college experience that nearly everyone else had done superior work in high school. The freshman's inability to achieve superior grades in college as easily as he had done in high school comes as a severe blow to some students' self-image. The budding professor, however, is usually the student who has continued to achieve high grades in college; hence, the undermining of his sense of unique superiority is postponed until he undertakes an academic career, at which point (at a relatively mature age), he is confronted for the first time with the fact that there are a lot of others who have always been the "brightest boy," a realization which is bound to threaten his self-esteem. One way in which this self-image can be defended, according to Stinchcombe, is through excessive criticism and derogation of others' work, as well as through backbiting, that is, developing excessive hostility toward his colleagues, particularly those who adhere to schools of thought that conflict with his own [Stinchcombe, 1963].

Another basic reason for insults among academicians, according to Stinchcombe, is the inherent conflict between the extreme individualism and pride that is associated with being intellectual, as opposed to the necessity for academics to work together as part of a department and to be collectively associated with an institution.

Insult among academics, particularly high-prestige professors, can be found in nearly every issue of national journals. Letters to the editor columns and review symposia are full of scathing comments and diatribes. Very often such insults and counterinsults are set off by negative reviews of one or the other party's latest book. Witness the following encounter between two of the biggest "names" in sociology that took place in a review symposium in *Contemporary Sociology* (A's review of B's book):

Like a short story writer who has decided the time has come to write his version of the Great American Novel, B the essayist had decided to turn his talents to producing a *magnus opus* [sic] . . . .

What is greatly missing is an integrating conception, a grand idea, an historical imagination which would help answer the crucial question: What are the social forces moving us and where are they headed? Instead, we have B's fascination with the obsolescent mode of *pre*-theorizing, as evidenced by his coining of new labels for social phenomena which already have quite solid and serviceable ones. . . .

As a book just published and dedicated to futurism, B's volume is already dated, not in this or that detail, but in several of its central themes. . . . B's view of the human species comes across as weary, fatigued. . . .

If to be an intellectual means to excel in eclecticism, to eschew overarching interpretations, to be utterly without dogma, and—at this stage in the decline of the old regime—to write with silenced hope and mounting weariness, then B clearly qualifies as one of America's greatest.

B's reply:

One point of personal privilege before a synoptic reply to the issues. . . . Mr. A writes of my "obsolescent mode of pre-theorizing by coining new labels, when our patience for such work has been exhausted. . . ." How extraordinary. There is no such word as *pre*-theorizing, underlined or not; it is a new label without sense. Mr. A's effort to substitute two different pairs for the terms I used are not congruent with the distinctions I was making. And Mr. A's "exhausted patience," coming from a man who has contributed more polyzoic strings to polysemiac terms to the sociological vocabulary than any other contemporary didact, only merits the rebuke, "quel chutzpah. . . ."

I do not think the concepts will arise from A's "broad-based coalition of all the numerous and various groups whose basic human needs cannot be met. . . ." (What precision of terms! . . . what elegance of language!)

Reviewers should not pick up catch phrases and try to use them as bludgeons. They end up as boomerangs.

Such exchanges of sharply critical, even insulting reviews and counterinsults are quite common in professional journals. Most often they take place between prominent figures, each of whom has laid claim to the position of highest eminence in a particular subfield or specialty within a discipline. The above gentlemen, for example, had both written lengthy attempts to set forth the future direction of American society, and thus both had claim to the informal position of highest eminence in that particular line of sociological endeavor. Unfortunately, it often happens that the scholar most qualified to review a book in a special area happens to be a prestige-rival of the writer. Because of this, book reviews often turn into insult games between academic titans, who, rather than objectively reviewing each other's work, use the review as a vehicle for deflating one another's status. More significantly, however, insult may often serve as a means of deflating the pretensions of scholars who present unfounded or unclear generalizations as scientific truth. In the long run, by pricking and perhaps even exploding the balloons of glory ("one of the most seminal thinkers of our age") that often appear on dustjackets of the books of major figures, insult among productive scholars, like insult against democratic politicians, may well prevent such figures from believing that they are "above" the humanity and the reality which they examine as scholars.

11

INSULT, AGGRESSION, AND WAR

Insult behavior is related to aggression and war in several significant ways. Insults can constitute both a form of aggression and a means whereby more serious aggression can be controlled. In some cultures, insult serves as a safety valve which allows people to vent aggressive attitudes in a nonlethal manner. In other contexts, however, insult often serves as a prelude and precipitant to overt, violent conflict. In this chapter we will compare these often paradoxically contrasting functions of insult behavior in a variety of sociocultural milieux.

Ritualized Insult as a Safety Valve

In some cultures patterns of ritualized insult allow for the expression of aggressive feelings and antagonistic attitudes without the danger and disruption of overt violence. In many tribal-village societies, such ritualized aggression is based upon supernaturalistic beliefs which, in effect, allow for the ritualistic "exorcism" of hostile feelings. In Iran, for example, there are two small villages separated by a ravine whose inhabitants gather periodically on both sides and, without any preliminaries, begin to exchange the crudest insults imaginable. After a certain period of time, they become reconciled again as if nothing had happened. This expression of hostile feeling has both a social and a religious function: it allows the villagers to live close together without overt conflict, and it is regarded as necessary to keep away bad luck [Masse, 1938:156]. In a similar manner, the Pukapukan people of the South Seas engage in a form of ritualized chanting which, according to the ethnographer Beaglehole, is a prime factor explaining their relatively low incidence of actual warfare and violence:

The composition and recitation [of the chants] provide a channelizing of emotion that might otherwise break out in less desirable, even antisocial ways. Sentiments of aggression in the individual and in groups of individuals are given an outlet in the taunting and boasting chants, and pass off in a great burst of harmless energy instead of banking up and flooding through channels of violence and homicide. This is a very necessary safeguard to develop in a small, closely confined community ... the practice of composing and singing chants ... has provided a socially approved outlet for feelings of aggression and hatred [Beaglehole and Beaglehole, 1953:89].

Does ritualized insult always serve as a preventative for the outbreak of overt hostility? The traditional Aleutian culture, according to an early ethnographic account, exhibited a pattern of ritual insult which served as a prelude and a precipitant to violence rather than as a safety valve for heading it off. The Aleuts had a game or entertainment for which the rivals made substantial preparations: composing and arranging songs and dances of a reproachful, abusive, and derisive nature. After a feast, the party began with the songs and dances; but gradually, underlying feelings of genuine antagonism would undermine the gamelike character of the ritual and lead to outbreaks of hostility and violence, sometimes even to homicide [Veniaminov, 1840:56].

Are there equivalents of the gamelike forms of tribal-village ritualized insult in modern societies? In many respects, institutionalized sports perform similar functions for modern peoples as ritualized insult games serve for many tribal-village societies. As William James [1895] suggested in his famous essay "The Moral Equivalent of War," sports are a prime means whereby societies might develop and emphasize the moral virtues associated with war: honor, courage, prowess, and so on, without the lethality of actual warfare. Moreover, sports allow spectators and fans to vent a good deal of aggressive emotion in identifying with and cheering for a team. Such intense fervor is functionally similar to nationalistic patriotism in times of war, and can provide a harmless outlet for the kinds of hostility and antagonism otherwise associated with actual war.

While most sports events involving team competition do function in a socially positive manner to drain off aggressive emotions, the limits of the formalized structure of institutionalized sports can sometimes be transgressed by the development of overzealousness among fans. There have been many soccer matches between Latin American teams in which spectators became so excited that riots, sometimes involving fatalities, erupted. In the United States, fans of competing teams have occasionally been known to engage in fighting and other disruptive behavior. In a recent article in the *New York Times* it was pointed out that many sports fans are no longer content with verbal insults against the players and fans of the opposite team, but have actually thrown bottles and other dangerous objects at players, and engaged in brawls with other spectators [Cady, 1975:31-32]. Although the article attributes this increasing tendency toward rowdyism to the large amounts of beer that many fans consume, it is nevertheless a good example of the manner in which institutionalized forms of ritualized conflict provide a release for aggressive emotion and can precipitate rather than drain off such collective hostile tendencies. Thus, while the provision of means for the expression of antagonism through insult often functions to prevent overt violence, it can also backfire, arousing underlying tensions so as to lead to actual conflict.

Insult as a Precipitant of War

Insult behavior is related to the instigation and perpetration of war in several ways. Just as insults have often served as a basis for interpersonal fighting, insults against a nation or its leaders can serve and have served as precipitants of overt hostility between nations. Perhaps one of the most famous examples of international insult which led to war was the "Zimmermann Telegram" intercepted by the British on January 17, 1917. The coded message was an offer from the Germans to restore to Mexico, in exchange for a martial alliance against the United States, territory which she had recently lost to the United States. President Wilson reacted to this serious affront to the then-neutral United States with fierce indignation, and the United States entered the war against Germany soon after.

Insults in the form of propaganda have also constituted an important mechanism for motivating one nation to engage in war with another. Although they did not precipitate actual warfare, the large amounts of propaganda released by the United States and the Soviet Union after World War II were largely responsible for the cold war. A Radio Moscow news broadcast of October 8, 1949, is typical of many such propagandized news releases of that time:

By smuggling Iranian foodstuffs out of this country, American officials have brought starvation to many parts of Iran.... The refusal of the American Government to assist the hungry Iranian people once again shows American imperialism in all its repulsive ugliness.... The American imperialists and their servile Iranian lackeys have thrown Iran into the grips of a horrible famine [Whitton and Larson, 1964:107].

Because of the close causal relationship between insult/propaganda and actual warfare, many nations rely on international peace agreements as well as norms of diplomacy to discourage communication to or about other nations which may incite a desire for war. The Geneva Convention Concerning the Use of Broadcasting in the Cause of Peace (April 2, 1938), discourages radio transmissions "likely to harm good international understanding or statements the incorrectness of which is or ought to be known to the persons responsible for the broadcast." Some nations make specific agreements with nations (often geographic neighbors) with whom conflict may for some reason seem possible. Such agreements, for example, were made between Poland and Lithuania in 1938, and between India and Pakistan in 1948. Attacks on foreign diplomats are illegal in most countries, and since 1794 it has been considered libellous to insult a foreign minister in the United States [Whitton and Larson, 1964:147; 175].

There is usually a wide range of causal factors and tensions inherent in the outbreak of any overt conflict between modern industrialized societies. And we have already seen how insults on the international scale often serve as "triggering events" which can cause international tensions to become overt hostilities. But ethnographic studies of tribal-village and caste-estate societies also afford numerous examples of wars which were instigated, through not necessarily caused, by insults which one group has directed against another group and its leaders. Many such incidents of overt hostilities among primitive peoples are a direct result of the fact that insults against individuals are considered to be insults against that individual's entire kin group. The collectivization of response to insult which leads to actual intergroup warfare is related to the necessity of tribal groups to maintain their honor by demonstrating their willingness and ability to defend it.

Various anthropologists have observed how cannibalism is a form of insult which has led to warfare among the members of various tribal-village societies in the South Pacific. In the Easter Islands, for example,

cannibalism was closely associated with war; the victors feasted on the corpses of the defeated and killed prisoners to be eaten. . . . Legends tell of grown persons and children who were slaughtered during peace time by warriors craving human flesh. These acts were deeply resented by the relatives of the victims who took cruel revenge for the crime, which was considered a terrible insult to the family [Metraux, 1940: 151].

And among the Fiji Islanders,

the motive behind most of the cannibalism . . . seems to have been revenge. After a successful raid the bodies of captured enemies were trussed like pigs and steamed in large earth ovens used especially for this purpose. The bodies were called mbakola, a term still used to inflict the most deadly of insults, Informants say that there is no act more humiliating to the relatives of a fallen enemy than the consumption of his flesh by the victors [Thompson, 140: 10].

Thus, insult behavior is related to aggression in a number of basic ways. Insults are a type of aggressive behavior in themselves; they can often incite people to violence; and in many respects, including the extreme instance of cannibalism as insult, the violent behavior itself may well constitute an insult. From the ethnomethodological perspective, the relation between insult and aggression stems from the ways in which acts, remarks, or gestures break the delicate fabric of shared conceptions of social reality and thus become defined as insults. In such circumstances, whether in interactions between preliterate peoples or between modern nation-states, the unexpectedness of insults and the danger of their rending the social fabric both define insults as aggressive in themselves and often incite violent responses.

12

CONCLUSIONS

In this book we have examined a wide range of ways in which insult behavior is related to the definition and maintenance of social and cultural processes and institutions. What are the implications of this study, and what import might it have for the examination of social change?

An important thread running throughout this book has been the idea that what is socially and culturally functional is not necessarily "positive" in an ethical or moral sense. As Lewis Coser [1964] points out, social conflict—including war—has many positive aspects for groups and societies that engage in it, including the establishment of intragroup solidarity and the reaffirmation of values and norms. But at the same time, no one can deny the destructive effects that are concomitant with many kinds of social conflict. These same generalizations also apply to insult behavior. Very often insults can cause physical as well as psychological damage, since they so easily involve or lead to violence. And the type of social and cultural processes and patterns they help maintain are often unjust and arbitrary. Does this, then, leave us with an irredeemably cynical view of human interaction and sociocultural patterns?

One of the important aspects of insult behavior that has been emphasized in the foregoing study is the possibility for social change to take place as the result of relevant changes in the patterns of response to insult. Recent efforts by minority groups to redress age-old grievances constitute a stalwart refusal to accept various acts, remarks, and characterizations of minorities which are insulting. With the rise of egalitarian social systems many, if not most, of the formalized patterns of insult and humiliation against those low on the scale of social status have been eliminated. But while such patterns are not as overt as they once were, they still remain, as we have seen, in more subtle form. And the fact that many lower-class working people as well as others of low social status have, in the modern era, increasingly refused to "take any crap" from those of higher social standing has led to a greater degree of levelling in modern society. It is no longer acceptable for the wealthy and powerful openly to condescend toward their "inferiors": those so insulted will often refuse to tolerate such displays of arrogance. In particular, since the beginning of the modern Black Revolution during the 1950s increasing numbers of black people have refused to endure insults and to participate in their own humiliation: the shuffling "Yassur, Boss" who sad-cheerfully accepts any humiliations or insults directed at him has for the most part been replaced by the proud young black who takes pride in his or her own cultural heritage and reacts contemptuously and in kind to collective insults. Thus, while many patterns of insult and response may serve, as we have seen, to maintain inequality and injustice, there is substantial evidence that newly emergent patterns in both insult and response to insult can and have played an important role in the accomplishment of needed social changes.

BIBLIOGRAPHY

Ahmad, Zainal Abidin bin. "Malay Manners and Etiquette." *Journal of the Royal Asiatic Society, Malayan Branch*, 23 (1950), 43-74.

Allport, Gordon. *The Nature of Prejudice*. New York: Doubleday, Anchor Books, 1958.

Altman, Dennis. *Homosexual: Oppression and Liberation*. New York: Avon, 1971.

Ammar, Hamed. *Growing Up in an Egyptian Village*. London: Routledge and Kegan Paul, 1954.

Barton, Roy Franklin. *Ifugao Law*. Berkeley: University of California Press, 1919.

Bascom, William R. "The Principle of Seniority in the Social Structure of the Yoruba." *American Anthropologist*, n.s. 44 (1942), 37-46.

———. "Social Status, Wealth, and Individual Differences among the Yoruba." *American Anthropologist*, 53 (1951), 490-505.

———. "Yoruba Food." *Africa*, 21 (1951), 41-53.

Basedow, Herbert. *The Australian Aboriginal*. Adelaide: F. W. Preece, 1925.

Beaglehole, Ernest, and Pearl Beaglehole. "Myths, Stories, and Chants from Pukapuka," unpublished manuscript. Honolulu: Bernice P. Bishop Museum, 1953.

Belo, Jane. "Study of a Balinese Family." *American Anthropologist*, 38 (1936), 12-31.

Benedict, Ruth. "Thai Culture and Behavior," unpublished wartime study. Ithaca: Cornell University Southeast Asia Program, 1952.

Best, Elsdon. *The Maori*, vol. 1. Wellington: H. H. Tombs, 1924.

Blumer, Herbert, quoted in Buckley, Walter. *Sociology and Modern Systems Theory*. New York: Prentice-Hall, 1967.

Buck, Peter Henry. *The Coming of the Maori*. Wellington: Whitcomb and Tombs, 1952.

Bullough, Vern L. *The Subordinate Sex.* Urbana: University of Illinois, 1973.

Cady, Steve. "Rowdyism: Games Fans Play." *New York Times,* May 20, 1975, p. 31.

Campbell, J. K. *Honour, Family, and Patronage: A Study of Institutions and Moral Values in a Greek Mountain Community.* Oxford: Clarendon Press, 1964.

Cicourel, Aaron. *Method and Measurement in Sociology.* New York: Free Press, 1964.

Coser, Lewis. *The Functions of Social Conflict.* New York: Free Press, 1964.

Davis, Kingsley. "Jealousy and Sexual Property." *Social Forces,* 14 (March 1936), 395-405.

Davis, Philip, and Robert Hamelberg. "Collective Insults against Black Students," unpublished paper, Miami University, 1973.

Dollard, John. "The Dozens: Dialect of Insult." *American Imago,* 1 (1939), 1-21.

Dubois, J. A. *Hindu Manners, Customs, and Ceremonies.* Oxford: Clarendon Press, 1906.

Dumont, Louis. *Homo Hierarchicus.* Chicago: University of Chicago Press, 1970.

Erikson, Kai T. *Wayward Puritans.* New York: Wiley, 1966.

Evans-Pritchard, Edward Evan. "Witchcraft among the Azande." *Sudan Notes and Records,* 12 (1929), 163-249.

Firth, Raymond. *Economics of the New Zealand Maori.* Wellington: R. E. Owen, 1959.

Flanagan, Robert. *Maggot.* New York: Paperback Library, 1971.

Friedl, Ernestine. *Vasilika: A Village in Modern Greece.* New York: Holt, Rinehart, and Winston, 1963.

Garfinkel, Harold. *Studies in Ethnomethodology.* Englewood Cliffs, N. J.: Prentice-Hall, 1967.

Ghurye, Govind S. *Caste and Class in India.* Bombay: Popular Book Depot, 1950.

Gladwin, Thomas, and Seymour B. Sarason. *Truk: Man in Paradise.* New York: Wenner-Gren Foundation for Anthropological Research, 1953.

Gold, Ray. "Janitors versus Tenants: A Status-Income Dilemma." *American Journal of Sociology,* 57 (1952), 486-93.

Grattan, F. J. H. *An Introduction to Samoan Custom.* Apia: Samoan Publishing, 1948.

Hallowell, A. Irving. *Culture and Personality.* Philadelphia: University of Pennsylvania Press, 1955.

Hammond, Peter B. "Mossi Joking." *Ethnology,* 3 (1964), 259-67.

Hauswirth, Frieda. *A Marriage to India.* New York: Vanguard, 1930.

Henry, Jules. *Jules Henry on Education.* New York: Random House, 1971.

Hogbin, H. Ian. "Social Reaction to Crime: Law and Morals in the Schouten Islands, New Guinea." *Journal of the Royal Anthropological Institute of Great Britain and Ireland,* 68 (1938), 223-62.

Horowitz, Ruth, and Gary Schwartz. "Honor, Normative Ambiguity, and Gang Violence." *American Sociological Review,* 39 (April, 1974), 238-51.

Hulstaert, Gustav. *Marriage among the Nkundu.* Brussels: G. van Campenhout, 1928.

Hutton, John Henry. *Caste in India: Its Nature, Function, and Origins.* Bombay: Oxford University Press, 1951.

Jones, Livingston French. *A Study of the Thlingets of Alaska.* New York: Revell, 1914.

Kane, Harnett T. *Gentlemen, Swords, and Pistols.* New York: Morrow, 1951.

Kenyatta, Jomo. *Facing Mount Kenya: The Tribal Life of the Kikuyu.* London: Secker and Warburg, 1953.

Kluckhohn, Clyde. *Navaho Witchcraft.* Cambridge: Peabody Museum, Harvard University, 1944.

Kochman, Thomas. "Verbal Behavior among Ghetto Youth." *Transaction*, 3 (February, 1969), 27-34.

Kozol, Jonathan. *Death at an Early Age.* New York: Bantam, 1967.

Labov, William. "Rules for Ritual Insults." *Studies in Social Interaction*, ed. David Sudnow. New York: Free Press, 1972.

Lambert, H. E. *Kikuyu Social and Political Institutions.* London and New York: Oxford University Press, 1956.

LaTourette, Kenneth Scott. *The Chinese, Their History and Culture*, vol. 2. New York: Macmillan, 1934.

Lee, Dorothy D. "Greece." *Cultural Patterns and Technical Change*, ed. Margaret Mead. Paris: Unesco, 1953, 77-114.

Mace, David and Vera Mace. *Marriage East and West.* New York: Doubleday, Dolphin Books, 1960.

MacKenzie, D. R. *The Spirit-Ridden Konde.* London: Seeley and Service, 1925.

Mair, Lucy Philip. *An African People in the Twentieth Century.* London: G. Routledge and Sons, 1934.

Makal, Mahmut. *A Village in Anatolia.* London: Vallentine, Mitchell, 1954.

Malinowski, Bronislaw. *Crime and Custom in a Savage Society.* London: K. Paul, Trench, Trubner; New York: Harcourt, Brace, 1926.

———. *The Sexual Life of Savages in Northwestern Melanesia.* New York: Horace Liveright, 1929.

Marshall, Lorna. "Sharing, Talking, and Giving: Relief of Social Tensions among the Kung Bushmen," *Africa*, 31 (1961), 231–49.

Martin, Frederick. *The Junker Menace.* New York: Richard Smith, 1945.

Masse, Henri. *Persian Beliefs and Customs.* Paris: Librairie Orientale et Américaine, 1938.

Matza, David. *Delinquency and Drift.* New York: Wiley, 1964.

McCown, Chester C. "The Price of Blood." *Asia*, 22 (1922), 786-90.

McHugh, Peter. *Defining the Situation.* New York: Bobbs-Merrill, 1968.

Mead, Margaret. *Social Organization of Manua.* Honolulu: Bernice P. Bishop Museum, 1930.

Metraux, Alfred. *Ethnology of Easter Island.* Honolulu: Bernice P. Bishop Museum, 1940.

———. "Suicide among the Matako of the Argentine Gran Chaco." *American Indigena*, 3 (1943), 199-209.

Mitchell, James Clyde. *The Yao Village: A Study in the Social Structure of a Nyasaland Tribe.* Manchester: Manchester University Press, 1956.

Monteil, Charles Victor. *The Bambara of Segov and Kaarta: An Historical, Ethnographical and Literary Study of a People of the French Sudan.* Paris: La Rose, 1924.

Morrill, George P. "The Best White Friend Black Americans Ever Had." *Reader's Digest,* 99, no. 591 (July, 1971), 169-74.

Muller, Wilhelm. *Yap.* Hamburg: Friederichsen, 1917.

Nguyen Van Khoan. "De la prestation de serments chez les annamites (On the Taking of Oaths among the Annamese)." Institut Indochinois pour l'Etude de l'Homme, Bulletins et Travaux pour 1942, 5, fasc. 1 (1942), 147-61.

Perlmutter, Nathan. *A Bias of Reflections: Confessions of an Incipient Old Jew.* New Rochelle, N. Y.: Arlington House, 1972.

Pett, Saul. "Nixon Tells of His Work: A Life without Relaxing." *New York Times,* January 14, 1973, p. 38.

Pineda Giraldo, Roberto. *Aspects of Magic in La Guajira.* Bogota, 1950.

Plaut, Hermann. *Contributions to the Knowledge of the Island of Formosa.* Berlin: Königliche Friedrich-Wilhelms-Universität, Seminar für Orientalische Sprachen, Mittheilungen, 1903, pp. 28-62.

Poussaint, Alvin F. "Cheap Thrills that Degrade Blacks." *Psychology Today,* February, 1974.

Powdermaker, Hortense. *Life in Lesu: The Study of a Melanesian Society in New Ireland.* New York: Norton, 1933.

Puner, Helen W. *Freud: His Life and His Mind.* New York: Dell, 1959.

Rattray, Robert Sutherland. *Ashanti Law and Constitution.* Oxford: Clarendon Press, 1929.

———. *Ashanti Proverbs.* Oxford: Clarendon Press, 1916.

Ray, Verne F. *The Sanpoil and Nespelem: Salishan Peoples of Northeastern Washington.* Seattle: University of Washington Press, 1933.

Reichel-Dolmatoff, Gerardo. *The Kogi: A Tribe of the Sierra Nevada de Santa Maria, Colombia,* vol. 2. Bogota: Editorial Iqueima, 1951.

Rouilly, Marcel. *The Annamese Commune.* Paris: Presses Modernes, 1929.

Ruesch, Hans. *Top of the World.* New York: Harpers, 1950.

[Salesius-] Haas, Johann Gustav. *The Carolines Island Yap.* Berlin: W. Susserott, 1907.

Schultze, Leonhard. *In Namaland and the Kalahari.* Jena: Gustav Fischer, 1907.

Seitz, Don. *Famous American Duels.* New York: Crowell, 1929.

Shirokogorov, Sergei. *Social Organization of the Manchus.* Shanghai, 1924.

Smith, Dennis. *Report from Engine 82.* New York: New American Library, 1972.

Smith, Michael Garfield. *The Economy of Hausa Communities of Zaria.* London: Her Majesty's Stationery Office, 1955.

Smithson, Carma Lee. *The Havasupai Woman.* Salt Lake City: University of Utah Press, 1959.

Stair, John Bettridge. *Old Samoa.* London: Religious Tract Society, 1897.

Stevens, William. *Pistols at Ten Paces.* Boston: Houghton-Mifflin, 1940.

Stinchcombe, Arthur. "On Not Getting Hung Up." *Johns Hopkins Review,* fall 1963.

Suggs, Robert Carl. "Sex and Personality in the Marquesas." *Human Sexual Behavior*, ed. Robert Carl Suggs and Donald S. Marshall. New York: Basic Books, 1971, pp. 163-86.

Swanton, John Reed. "Social Organization and Social Usages of the Indians of the Creek Confederacy." U.S. Bureau of American Ethnology, *Annual Report*, 1924-25.

Tessmann, Gunter. *The Fang Peoples: An Ethnographic Monograph on a West African Negro Group*, vol. 2. Berlin: Ernst Wasmuth, 1913.

Thompson, Laura. *Southern Lau, Fiji: An Ethnography*. Honolulu: Bernice P. Bishop Museum, 1940.

Tuchman, Barbara. *The Zimmermann Telegram*. New York: Macmillan, 1966.

Turrado Moreno, Angel. *Ethnography of the Guarauno Indians*. Caracas: Vargas, 1945.

Vassal, Gabrielle. *On and Off Duty in Annam*. London: W. Heinemann, 1910.

Veniaminov, Ivan. *Notes on the Islands of the Unalaska District*. Saint Petersburg: Izdano Izhdiveniem Rossiisko-Amerikanskoi Kompanii, 1840.

Warner, W. Lloyd. *A Black Civilization: A Social Study of an Australian Tribe*. New York: Harper, 1937.

Whiting, Beatrice Blyth. *Paiute Sorcery*. New York: Viking Fund, 1950.

Whitman, William. *The Pueblo Indians of San Ildefonso: A Changing Culture*. New York: Columbia University Press, 1947.

Whitton, John B., and Arthur Larson. *Propaganda: Towards Disarmament in the War of Words*. Dobbs Ferry, N.Y.: Oceana Publications, Inc., 1964.

Winstedt, Richard Olof. *Papers on Malay Subjects, Life and Customs*. Kuala Lumpur: Federated Malay States Government Press, 1925.

Wittenberg, Philip. *Dangerous Words: A Guide to the Law of Libel*. New York: Columbia University Press, 1947.

X, Malcolm. *The Autobiography of Malcolm X*. New York: Grove Press, 1966.

Yang, Mou-Chun. *A Chinese Village: Taitou, Shantung Province*. New York: Columbia University Press, 1945.

Young, Stephen M. *Tales out of Congress*. Philadelphia and New York: J. B. Lippincott, 1964.

INDEX